So far in my political life, I haven't had the misfortune to be confronted by the Raging Grannies in full throttle. *Off Our Rockers* gives me ample reason to hope I never make a good target for them. As this immensely readable book proves, the Grannies are a force to be reckoned with — courageous, outrageous and very funny.

— Ed Broadbent, former federal
leader of the New Democratic Party

Off Our Rockers says so much about the power of women who believe humorous, sometimes obnoxious, unladylike behaviour can make a change. Feistiness, smartness and courage leap off these pages in a no-nonsense style. Here's proof that a small group of ordinary women can become extraordinary through their passion and commitment. Buy this book. It rocks.

— Lorna Crozier, winner of a Governor General's
Literary Award in 1992

If Canada is about peace, order and good government, then the Grannies are for peace, disorder and good fun. *Off Our Rockers* will scratch the Canadian funny bone.

— The Honourable Lloyd Axworthy,
former minister of foreign affairs and
president of the University of Winnipeg

Fearless, outrageous, marvellous — these Grannies tell it like it is as few others do. I hope these role models inspire imitators from my gender too.

— David Suzuki

OFF OUR ROCKERS

and into trouble

The Raging Grannies

y are here for the ... we cannot sleep in peace

you like living dangerously, call ... e command

ALISON ACKER   BETTY BRIGHTWELL

TouchWood Editions Ltd.
Victoria, BC, Canada
This book is distributed by The Heritage Group, #108-17665 66A Avenue, Surrey, BC, Canada, V3S 2A7.

Cover and interior design: Ronan Lannuezel, Marketing Dynamics. Production: Nancy St.Gelais and Darlene Nickull. Front-cover photo: Bruce Stotesbury, Victoria *Times Colonist* (colour detail of inside photo). Back-cover photo: *The Ottawa Citizen* (use of this photo does not imply support by *The Ottawa Citizen* of The Raging Grannies or any of their causes, political or otherwise).
Editor: Marlyn Horsdal.

This book is set in Adobe Garamond Pro.

TouchWood Editions acknowledges the financial support for its publishing program from The Canada Council for the Arts, the Government of Canada through the Book Publishing Industry Development Program (BPIDP) and the Province of British Columbia through the British Columbia Arts Council.

Printed in Canada on forest-friendly, 100% recycled paper.

National Library of Canada Cataloguing in Publication

Acker, Alison, 1928-
      Off our rockers and into trouble: the Raging Grannies / Alison Acker and Betty Brightwell. — 1st ed.

Includes bibliographical references and index.
ISBN 1-894898-10-9

      1. Raging Grannies. 2. Aged women — Political activity — Canada. 3. Protest movements — Canada. I. Brightwell, Betty, 1925-   II. Title.

HQ1236.A32 2004   361.2'3'08460971   C2004-901396-3

BRITISH
COLUMBIA
ARTS COUNCIL

The Canada Council | Le Conseil des Arts
for the Arts | du Canada

This book is dedicated
to the grandchildren
of the world.

FOREWORD

It took a long time to get *Off Our Rockers* into your hands. An earlier group attempt at writing the history of the Raging Grannies was abandoned in 1993 after the Victoria Grannies could not agree on its style. We built *Off Our Rockers* on the foundation laid by that first effort, bolstered by old minute books, scribbled calendar entries, one Granny's faithful diary, newspaper clippings and our sometimes failing memories. Some years earlier we had had the sense to offer our ephemera to the Women's Studies Archives at the University of Victoria. We happily ate their cookies and drank their tea during the accession ceremony. So there were some facts we were sure of because they were in the archives.

This time we had only two authors, who let me edit their work. Long after I thought the book was done, one of them would tell an anecdote and I would wail, "That has to be in the book." Only the deadline set by our publisher put an end to the revisions.

We three began work on *Off Our Rockers* in 2001, which forced Alison Acker to get her first computer. Betty Brightwell had been wired for years. At a chance meeting at a yoga class, TouchWood Editions' Marlyn Horsdal expressed a polite interest in seeing the manuscript. We assured her we had lots of friends and relatives who would buy the book. It took two years for *Off Our Rockers* to hit her desk. We had pre-sold eight advance copies to out-of-town Grannies; the money was in the bank, so we had to deliver.

Meanwhile, the other Victoria Grannies had the tact not to keep asking when the book would be ready and the forbearance to refrain from demanding to approve the text.

We are grateful to Grannies far and wide who provided such wonderful antics to write about and to the politicians, warmongers and corporate tycoons whose silly decisions made them sitting ducks for our songs and actions. We also thank the numerous librarians, archivists, peace and environmental groups and just plain folks who helped us get it right, we hope. Any errors are ours — and we apologize in advance.

Anne Moon, Project Coordinator

CONTENTS

THE RAGING GRANNIES - VICTORIA'S SECRET?

Once we were invisible. Like all older women, we were expected to fade into the background along with our looks, our health, our income and our importance to society. But not any more. This is the story of a group of women in Victoria, British Columbia, who decided to break the stereotype of nice but negligible grandmothers by becoming outrageous.

We were out to shock. We would dress up as crazy old ladies in extravagant hats to get attention and then we would really make a noise. We would rattle the cages of all those who, we felt, were destroying our world: politicians, corporations, warmongers and wreckers of the environment.

Like court jesters, we would use humour to mock the mighty, but we would not be on anyone's payroll. We would go where we were not invited and sing out loud what was not supposed to be said. We would be guerrilla singers and we would change the world, so there! Heady dreams indeed.

Strangely enough, we haven't changed the world or accomplished any miracles in the 17 years since we formed the Victoria Raging Grannies. In reality, the world has gotten nastier in spite of us. Sure, we've ruffled a few feathers, gotten a lot of media coverage, annoyed many Canadian citizens and delighted some others, but the differences we have made are largely in raising awareness. You might call us whistle-blowers, catalysts, troublemakers, general nuisances. In our own peculiar fashion, we've worked for peace and nuclear disarmament, safe food and water, saving the forests and an end to poverty, homelessness, injustice and war — sometimes on our own, sometimes with larger groups. It's been a rough ride, with few victories, but we've had a lot of fun on the way.

We hope we've opened some eyes and shaken up the complacent. We like to think we are a thorn in the side of authority and, we hope, an example of ordinary people making a difference. When we get downhearted, which isn't often, we remember Margaret Mead, the anthropologist, and her conviction that a small group of thoughtful, committed citizens can change the world. And, she added, it is the only thing that ever has.

Perhaps our greatest success has been in something we never intended — the spread of the Raging Granny concept to more than 60 groups stretching across Canada and the United States and reaching into the United Kingdom, Europe, even Australia. Without any attempt to start a movement, we did it, so we must be doing something right. Take a look at the website — www.geocities.com/raginggrannies/ — emblazoned with a symbolic Granny, umbrella raised on high, and see Grannies everywhere, making themselves heard. We're out there and we're growing.

One secret of our group's success is that we do so enjoy being Grannies. We laugh a lot together, about our own "senior moments" and impractical brainstorms. We meet once a week to plan actions and to rehearse. We eat out together often and take off together for retreats in borrowed cabins by the sea. Best of all, we travel to gigs or to meet other Grannies at regional gatherings or the more formal national Unconventions. There's something about

Victoria Grannies Betty, Fran, Jean, Ria, Alison and Inger (left to right) head down Douglas Street toward the legislature in an annual peace march.

a road trip with the Grannies that brings out the secret Thelma and Louise in us all.

No, we're not running away and we're not armed, but we might be dangerous. We're freer on the road, wilder, more adventurous. That may be because of our travel style — on the cheap, packed tight in cars, sometimes sleeping in tents, sometimes as many as eight to a room or in hostel bunk beds. Those with the weakest bladders get the bottom bunks. We get lost on the road. We make too much noise in restaurants and tip excessively to make up for our bad behaviour. We flirt with gas jockeys. We laugh so hard we need to pee. We stay up late and tell secrets about our wicked pasts. We eat far too much and feel marvellous.

Watch out for us if you are on the road. Ours are the cars pasted with bumper stickers about saving the world, spilling over with gear and Grannies and silly hats.

We make no apologies for enjoying ourselves while fighting for a cause, because laughter lightens the stress and holds us together. But in those early years we were very, very earnest. It was anger, rather than joy, that fuelled our fires at that inaugural meeting in Bess Ready's living room in Victoria, British Columbia, in April 1987.

"She may look like somebody's granny to you, but she helped to chase the nuclear-powered aircraft carrier out of our harbour."

NUCLEAR UMBRELLA

Lyrics and melody by
Jane Mackey

Beneath the nuclear umbrella
We're as safe as we can be.
Bush is such a lovely fella
He'll look after you and me.
We don't have to think about it.
Our defence has been assured.
What would we all do without it?
Don't it make you feel secure!
[Grannies open an umbrella full of holes]

IN THE BEGINNING

Time and trouble will tame an advanced young woman, but an advanced old woman is uncontrollable by any earthly force.
— Dorothy Sayers

en women, most of us members of the Greater Victoria Disarmament Group, had already talked about the need for a new image and new aims — a new type of street theatre that would grab attention for issues that made the world seem more and more dangerous. When clouds from the accident in a nuclear reactor at Chernobyl in the Soviet Union in April 1986 spread across Europe, we truly wondered if we would see the end of the world as we knew it. It was time to stop moaning and take action. Yes, we were mad as hell about a lot of things. We certainly made enough noise, with Sophie, Bess's aging and indignant poodle, adding to the din.

The 1980s had not brought the peace and justice we had all been led to expect when the Cold War ended. This was the world of Chernobyl and Grenada, of Maggie Thatcher, AIDS and the ozone layer, of designer jeans and addicted teens and a nuclear threat still hanging over us all. This was supposed to be the age of disarmament, but nuclear-weapons bases still flourished. Women in England were besieging the gates of the missile base at Greenham Common to protest and were getting arrested daily. There had to be something we could do, even in a relative backwater like Victoria.

Since we were all involved in the peace movement anyway, that seemed a good place to become assertive about all the things we wanted to change. We had become aware that it was men who had created nuclear weapons and still clung to them, and largely it was women who protested them. We couldn't help but connect the patriarchal establishment with those pointy warheads that they loved so much. Some of us were more wrapped up in women's rights than others, and one was heard to bellow that patriarchy was responsible for all the ills of the world. Most of us recognized the limitations imposed on our lives as women, especially when we were growing up and facing the three main career options: nursing, teaching or office work.

Many of us had a lot of anger still bottled up inside, even though we had, indeed, found satisfying careers. We'd had reasonably good marriages, many kids and grandchildren, but we wanted more from our lives. We wanted to make a difference. Getting older reminded us that we hadn't a lot of time, so we'd better get busy. And if we wanted to change society, we'd have to change our methods, because they weren't working.

Sending petitions or writing letters to the government merely produced the usual platitudes in response and made us feel even angrier. We seemed to direct a lot of our enmity toward both provincial and federal governments. Betty Brightwell figures that had something to do with the predominance of socialists in the peace movement and in our own group. Alison Acker thinks they were simply the natural targets because they had the power. We often agreed to disagree.

"We need to show up the politicians," howled a woman fed up with Bill Vander Zalm, then premier of British Columbia, and his Social Credit Party that had swung our province back to the right after a period of New Democratic Party government.

"They are letting down the very people who elected them," said another, shaking her fist.

"And they don't listen to us. It's ageism. Nobody respects the opinions of wise old grandmothers."

"You mean raging old ladies," added someone who wasn't a grandmother.

"That's it. We need a name. Let's call ourselves raging grandmothers."

"We'll be the Raging Grannies!"

The way the shouting and anger was progressing, any one of us might have shouted it. Doran Doyle and Fran Thoburn both insist they said the magic words. As Doran put it later, "We were women who kept meeting each other at rallies, women who were angry, but who weren't sure if it was okay to be angry. We began to realize that anger was an appropriate emotion for the mess that was being made of our world, and that being Grannies gave us both a freedom and a responsibility to do something about our anger." Doran was fond of quoting the holy words of the Catholic feminist writer Mary Daly: "Rage is not a stage, it is a transformative, focusing force."

Others saw their "raging" more as an external attitude that contradicted the stereotype of the sweet little old lady. Never mind philosophies; the issue that first brought us together was fear of annihilation. American warships, armed with nuclear weapons, had begun arriving regularly in our waters, docking at Esquimalt Naval Base, the National Defence headquarters of Canada's Maritime Forces Pacific (MARPAC), just outside Victoria, or continuing to the weapons-testing site at Nanoose Bay, Canadian Forces Maritime Experimental Test Range (CFMETR), 120 kilometres up Vancouver Island.

We also thought Brian Mulroney's Progressive Conservative government too compliant with NATO and ready to give our sovereignty away. Bill Vander Zalm was an avid accomplice, continuing the 30-year-old Social Credit policy of favouring corporations, especially the large forestry companies intent on clear-cutting Vancouver Island. Fortunately, both were ideal fodder for the cartoonists, and theirs was the method we would emulate — the use of laughter to ridicule vice and folly. Targets were everywhere, waiting for our slings and arrows. We all knew Marshall McLuhan's dictum, "The medium is the message," and being Raging Grannies in frumpy clothes and tasteless hats was to become the medium for our message.

We outlined our aims:

a) To inspire older women to be activists.
b) To deal with survival issues.
c) To get the message across with satiric songs.
d) To court the media.
e) To adopt Canadian author Margaret Laurence's prescription: "As we grow older we should become not less radical but more so."[1]
f) To remain independent of other organizations.
g) To be a support group for each other.
h) To be rabble-rousers.

At first, our issues revolved around war, especially the visits of atomic-powered and nuclear-armed ships to British Columbia, but we also opposed uranium mining in B.C., the storage of nuclear waste and the use of nuclear power of any sort. We wanted to support First Nations in their struggles for self-determination. We were all for environmentally safe logging and environmentally sound toilet paper. We were mad at the closing of Victoria's free Emily Carr Art Gallery, since the Art Gallery of Greater Victoria demanded entrance fees. We worried about housing for the poor, hot lunches for hungry kids and better treatment for Victoria's street people. We didn't like the city's dumping of raw sewage in the ocean; we bothered our heads about chlorofluorocarbon production and even learned how to pronounce it.

Then there were NAFTA, NORAD and the FTAA — a whole alphabet soup of questionable organizations that we didn't trust. And what about corporate globalization and sweatshops! Soon we'd have the Gulf War, the Balkan War, Palestine and Israel, then Afghanistan and Iraq to worry about. But back at that first meeting, we really had no idea what we were taking on. We never thought we were starting a movement that would spread around the world. Like Topsy, we just grew.

One of the women at that heady meeting, Moira Walker, would leave us, saying her busy life did not give her sufficient time to devote to Grannying. Jane Mackey stayed with us for the first two years and her songs became the signature of the Grannies. She wrote our songs and was our musical leader. A glance at the rest of the originals — Bess, Betty, Doran, Fran, Hilda, Jane, Joyce, Linda, Lois and Mary — gives some idea of the calibre of the first Raging Grannies. (Hilda was not at that first meeting but was definitely part of the group.)

Bess Ready grew up on a Manitoba farm and trained as a nurse at a time when nurses received no pay; her mother had to make her uniform. She nursed war casualties in Britain's famous Basingstoke Burn Hospital in World War II. She married a university librarian

This is an early picture of us in our thrift-store finery, taken on Bess Ready's back porch. Back row, left to right: Mary, Joyce, Lois, Doran. Front row: Jane, Fran, Hilda, Betty.

and author, became more politicized by her time in the United States during the McCarthy era and joined the Greater Victoria Disarmament Group when she came to Victoria. An accomplished artist, Bess painted everyday objects like shoes and feet as well as landscapes, and many of us have her paintings hung with pride in our homes. She has always been a great performer, our leader in street theatre, climbing onto the stage with her walker in later years, much to the delight of audiences. Now in the "independents" wing of Oak Bay Lodge, a seniors' residence, and well into her 80s, she still swims, plays bridge and is involved in the social life of her residence. She hasn't lost her Granny moxie, either. When two of us visited her too late for tea and cookies, Bess marched through the door marked "Staff Only" and rummaged through the kitchen until she found a plate of sandwiches, probably meant for the kitchen workers. "Here, take these," said Bess. "You have to do things for yourself round here."

Betty Brightwell came to meetings wearing pearls. Some Grannies thought she was a spy for the CIA; she was, indeed, quite nervous to find herself sitting down with socialists. Her Tide-white gloves confirmed her heritage as a seventh-generation upper-crust Canadian, so guess who was surprised to find that her great-great-grandfather had marched down Toronto's Yonge Street in support of William Lyon Mackenzie's 1837 Rebellion? During World War II Betty worked as an electrician's helper at a North Vancouver shipyard for two university summers, which opened her eyes to the working world, but then she married an air force officer and followed him from base to base.

The military world soon left her disenchanted. It became clear to both her husband and herself during the Cuban missile crisis of 1962 that it was American generals, sitting on their butts in Colorado Springs, who directed the Canadian forces; they, rather than Canada's prime minister, put Canada's military on yellow alert.

When he retired, her husband joined the Veterans Against Nuclear Arms and the World Federalists. Betty went to the first Victoria Peace Walk, where she met Hilda and was invited to take part in an upcoming protest outside the gates of the Canadian Forces Base in Esquimalt, a suburb of Victoria. She didn't go, but she did drive by, honking her car horn and waving. And she went to the next meeting of Extenuating Circumstances, the street-theatre group that preceded the Grannies, "putting on a nice dress and wearing my gold chains and earrings and bracelets and feeling quite out of place." But she soon found her place, especially in dealing with the press and with officials, where her image of respectability comes in very handy.

Protesting visits of nuclear warships has always been Betty's main concern, and it is sometimes hard for her to go along with the other issues that Grannies espouse. "Count me out," says Betty. But then she shows up at the next anti-poverty rally.

Betty is a connoisseur and collector of antiques. She is always talking about selling some of them so there would be more space in her living room, but if she goes to an antique show she comes back with more. She has been a teacher and a farmer, enlightening us with the gory details of difficult deliveries in the cow barn. She is also a local-history buff, having contributed to two books on the subject, and takes her civic duties seriously. She has run for council and come in last — her platform of eliminating visits by U.S. nuclear warships wasn't a winner in a naval town. She has been on boards, even been a member of the Esquimalt cycling committee, though she hasn't been on a bike in years. She is the nightmare of local developers. Recently, a municipal worker chopping down a tree met up with Betty, who was walking her ancient but beloved poodle, Muffin (who has since died). She spotted him and was about to thunder forth about the evils of development and the sacredness of trees when he mumbled, "Oops! You must be Betty. They told me I ought to talk to you first!"

Betty is a computer whiz, the first of us to get onto the Internet, and now an expert in digital photography, which enables her to immortalize our protests in the alternative press worldwide — and capture evidence of any police misbehaviour, too. She learned early the thrills and dangers of starting petitions when she decided to "Save the CBC" in the mid-'90s and got flooded with 30,000 signatures that had to be printed up and bundled into packages to go to Victoria MP David Anderson and then to Perrin Beatty, chair of the Canadian Broadcasting Corporation at the time. Though the CBC got saved and Betty got a CBC T-shirt for her pains, she won't do that again. But Victoria did get its own CBC radio station shortly afterward.

Doran Doyle was born in New Zealand. A Catholic feminist who rebelled against the paternalism of the church, Doran was the one who got everybody reading about rage and how good it was for all of us women. It was Doran who made reluctant Grannies take off their shoes and dance barefoot on her lawn to honour nature. She was proud to be called a witch, and at first many Grannies were somewhat afraid of her. But she was also the only one of us with any real experience in confronting authority, so we respected her. It was Doran who had lived with the women on Greenham Common and carried the pliers used to bend the wire so that they could sneak into the missile site. She was our driving force in the early years. Doran started Victoria's weekly downtown interfaith peace vigil and it was she who had most of our bright ideas. One time she persuaded us all to go to a forest company open house wearing bright green wool over our faces to show how we'd all had the wool pulled over our eyes. We don't think anybody got the message, but it was a tribute to her that we took up her idea.

Doran was dynamic and so was her fashion sense. Although married to a University of Victoria professor and living in an upscale neighbourhood among rhododendrons and roses, she always seemed much happier dressed as the lady who ran off with the Raggle Taggle Gypsies-O, typically outfitted for Granny events with scarves, flowers, ribbons and bells flying from an air force jacket topped off with a bus-driver's hat. When she moved to a sheep farm in the Cowichan Valley to live the simple life, she left the Grannies. However, she is still active in environmental issues and was recently sighted at a rally attired as the ocean.

Fran Thoburn was born in Cleveland, Ohio, on Leap Year Day, 1932, which makes her by far our youngest Granny in years and shortchanges her on birthdays. Her maternal great-grandmother had been a suffragette and had helped runaway slaves travelling the underground railroad to Canada before the Civil War. Her maternal grandmother had smuggled birth-control items from England to distribute among poor women. Her father was raised in a Methodist missionary home. Fran learned how to argue with him at the dinner table and went to university intending to become a doctor but was told, "We don't like to give women a medical education because they will just get married and have children." And that's what she did. She left university, married a private in the U.S. Army, followed him to Germany (defying the army rules of no wives overseas) and had four children.

Back in the U.S. she became active in the civil-rights movement and the anti-Vietnam War protests. She got a degree in psychology and a teaching certificate and the family headed to Toronto, where she helped start the Toronto Women's Health Centre and trained as a paramedic, working to empower street women as well as treat them.

In 1970 she left her husband for another expatriate American; they moved to the country, built their own house and lived off the land. In 1985 she had had enough of marriage — "bringing up four children and two husbands," as she described it — and moved to Victoria, where she wrote and produced a weekly half-hour show on peace issues for the University of Victoria radio station.

Fran now has six grandchildren and a standard poodle. She is an ardent dog lover, usually bringing her dog on protest marches, which she attends even when she has to come on crutches because of numerous foot and knee injuries. Having to use crutches is hard, after a very active life, including a hike in the Himalayas, but she's a tough cookie.

Hilda Marczak is a woman of fierce convictions; they were born of memories of her parents talking about pogroms against the Jews and her own experiences of anti-Semitism and police attacks on unemployed protesters during the Depression in Montreal. As early as high school, she joined the picket line when students were told they had to buy their textbooks. From there she went on to picket an aircraft factory when there was a strike. During World War II she became "Rosie the Riveter," working on munitions and volunteering at a hospitality centre for refugees, where she met her future husband. They moved to Victoria, where they both continued their efforts for peace during the Cold War, helping to collect 10,000 names in less than three weeks for one peace petition.

A great performer and a former kindergarten teacher, Hilda tried and tried to get the Grannies to sing at the same time on the same note and to put the left foot in and the right foot out, but all in vain. We must have been very much a disappointment, but Hilda soldiered on and it was her wisdom that enabled her to found Victoria's Middle East Peace Coalition before the first war in the Persian Gulf in 1990.

Jane Mackey was born in Washington, D.C., and became involved in the civil-rights movement very early. At 16, she was on the picket line to protest housing conditions in the largely Black downtown after a child died of lead poisoning. At the University of Montana, she became part of the anti-war and women's movements and a member of the Congress of Racial Equality (CORE). In the 1970s she married a Canadian and moved with him to the Kootenay area of the B.C. Interior, along with many Americans looking for a simpler, more self-sufficient way of life.

When they moved to Victoria in 1980, Jane worked as a counsellor and project organizer. It was as a member of Extenuating Circumstances, the street-theatre group, that she met the other original Grannies and attended that first seminal meeting. Though she had musical talent and loved making up rhymes, she never anticipated her role as composer of the satirical songs that would set the style for all Raging Granny groups. "Never preach," said Jane. And we don't.

Joyce Stewart grew up fighting for justice. Her father taught Japanese internees who had been removed from Canada's west coast to the Interior after Pearl Harbor. She insists she was a shy girl, but that shy girl became a corporal in World War II, flying beside the pilot as a spotter for downed aircraft off Vancouver Island. Married and with three children, she took charge of a reception centre for immigrants in Calgary and later helped found the Native Friendship Club there, receiving the Queen's Medal in 1977 for her services.

When her husband retired and they moved to Victoria, she worked at the Royal BC Museum and the Global Village store, and joined Project North (an inter-church coalition of solidarity with the First Nations), the Voice of Women, Veterans Against Nuclear Arms and then the Grannies. Joyce always took protesting seriously, chiding those who got carried away with silliness and providing a welcome sense of sanity and responsibility. But there have been times when passion broke through, as this account will show, and Grannies have whispered, "We never knew she had it in her." My, Joyce could be a surprise.

Linda Siegel was a member of Extenuating Circumstances before the Grannies began. Born in Rhode Island, U.S., she brought the snap of American energy to the Grannies, though her usual costume was more akin to mother of the bride — a peacock-blue lace dress with matching coat and a pair of white lace knickers hanging two inches below the hem. When the weather was cold, she wore a red mohair coat that made her look like a hairy bear.

We soon learned never to call her a lady. Linda was a serious feminist, proud of being assertive. The only child of older, Jewish parents, she grew up relating more to the poorer kids on the other side of the tracks than to her respectable neighbours, and she carried her concern for social justice and equal rights throughout her career as a teacher and counsellor. Even when she moved to Toronto and continued her work as a school counsellor, she still felt she was bucking the system. The Raging Grannies were to provide her with an outlet for her anger against injustice and a chance to act up. Though her grade-school teacher told her, "Please, never sing," she found she was no worse a singer than any other Granny and even better than some.

Lois Marcoux was quiet but one of our strongest Grannies. She always remembered the great drought in Saskatchewan in the Dirty Thirties when her parents had to struggle to keep the farm. Even now she can recall the wind that blew in under the door and lifted the linoleum day after day. She also remembers hearing her mother and her mother's three best friends, all former teachers, talking around the kitchen table about politics and family planning.

Lois got married, had seven children and many grandchildren and worked for years with the Catholic Diocese of Victoria on Project North. She has also worked with prisoners at William Head Penitentiary near Victoria, and with Conscience Canada to stop tax money being spent on armaments. It was all part of what she saw as acting out the Good News of the Gospel, which included protesting for peace by joining Hilda and Doran in 1986 in a 120-kilometre walk from Victoria to the Nanoose Bay weapons-testing base before the Grannies began.

Mary Rose's folk came over on the next boat after the *Mayflower* and she is a seventh-generation Canadian. However, she inherited her spirit of protest directly from her father, who was a travelling organizer for the Industrial Workers of the World (Wobblies). Off he went when Mary was six months old; the family didn't see him again until Mary's youngest child was four. Left in Victoria with four daughters to bring up, Mary's mother made do on mother's allowance, occasional work as a nurse and help from relatives. Mary remembers bundles of cast-off clothes arriving from Britain labelled Jaeger and Harris tweed. When money ran out, her mother would explain, "I like to keep my money in circulation."

Mary worked as an aircraft riveter and fitter on Sea Island, outside Vancouver, and as a bank teller before getting married. She moved with her husband to Ontario, where she studied art at Fanshawe College in London. Not only has she created many inspired and inspiring Granny banners, she has exhibited her work as far away as Argentina. She came to Victoria with her husband and they opened a smoke shop. Widowed in 1988, she remarried in 1993.

We weren't too taken with her new man, but he came with an enormous advantage — a house on Thetis Island with a solar-heated, saltwater swimming pool. Naturally, we fished for an invitation and descended *en masse*. That pool looked dazzling. Only a glass wall separated the pool from the sea, and it was possible to float naked and wave safely at passing ferries. Except that the master of the house was also in the pool, on a floating mattress, beer in hand, cap on head but otherwise naked. We hesitated very briefly and then dived in to join him. Not a word was said. Of course, he was English and knew that one remains invisible to others unless one has had an introduction. Pat and Mary have since separated. We hope it wasn't our fault. Now Mary is on her own again, living on Gabriola Island, across from Nanaimo, but still taking part in both her local Granny group and the Victoria group when she comes "down island" to visit her family.

We have always been surprised by Mary, who enjoys change and explains that she had lived in 13 different homes by the time she was 15 and was happiest "going with the flow." So if Mary joined the Progressive Conservative Party (to support David Orchard, an anti-free-trade right winger) or has had us watching the sky for "chem trails," which she insists are not aircraft contrails but part of the U.S. Defence Department's scheme of mind control, that's fine with us. We love her spirit of adventure.

So we were newly born Raging Grannies, committed to action, but of course we already had a number of actions under our belt from working in the peace movement — inspired actions indeed, though not always successful at getting our message across. And that's why we became Grannies — to make waves and make people listen.

Rest and Recreation

Sung to the tune of
"John Brown's Body," traditional; lyrics by Alison Acker

Every month the U.S. nuclear battleships drop by.
They're crewed by lovely fellas who would never hurt a fly.
But each of them could blow British Columbia sky high
'cos they're carrying nuclear bombs.

Chorus:
They're here for rest and recreation [x3]
But we cannot sleep in peace.

It's kind of George to send the ships so we can get a date.
With love boats coming into port, we too might find a mate.
But if he brings his toys along we'd really rather wait
'cos he's carrying nuclear bombs.

Chorus

If you like living dangerously, call the base command
Dial 363-2397 to get yourself a man.
But please remember, ladies, that there's no emergency plan
When you're carrying nuclear bombs.

Chorus

FINDING A VOICE

"Rage is not a stage,
it is a transformative, focusing force.
— *Mary Daly*

efore the Grannies began, there was Extenuating
Circumstances, a large theatre group formed to protest
nuclear-powered American naval ships' visits to Esquimalt
Harbour. It obtained its odd name when a Canadian Forces Base
open house was cancelled "due to extenuating circumstances."
Apparently the base commander got wind of the group's impending
arrival to protest the presence of a nuclear submarine.

In Victoria, during the height of the Cold War, peace activists
were protesting at Canadian Forces Base Esquimalt whenever a
nuclear submarine was in port. In 1986, the Greater Victoria
Disarmament Group paid an American professor to do a study
of the dangers the visits posed. The result was a document
entitled *Nuclear accidents on military vessels in Canadian ports,
site-specific analyses for Esquimalt/Victoria*, by W. Jackson Davis,
Ph.D., Professor of Biology, Nuclear Policy Program, University
of California at Santa Cruz, California. We were impressed! Davis
was asked to evaluate the consequences of hypothetical nuclear

accidents aboard military ships in both Esquimalt and Victoria and concluded: "Emergency preparedness for a nuclear accident in Canadian ports is inadequate. Civilian regulatory bodies exercise no licensing nor oversight authority over the technical aspects of U.S. military reactors and weapons. Without public knowledge of emergency preparedness plans, it is therefore not clear how public participation in a time of actual emergency could be implemented."[1]

We wanted to bring this to public attention because a serious fire on a nuclear-powered or nuclear-weapons-carrying ship in CFB Esquimalt could be disastrous. The prevailing west wind would blow radioactive fallout directly into the city, and evacuation would be impossible because there is only Highway 1 North as an escape route. A coolant leak from the nuclear operating system would pollute local waters, kill salmon and deter tourists, whilst the ultimate horror could be a nuclear explosion. It was only later, after protests from the Raging Grannies and other peace activists, that the Canadian Department of National Defence (DND) adopted a few safety measures at the base.

So, for an hour, we might stand on the pavement outside the naval base, holding up signs of protest and sweeping up "radiation" with brooms and feather dusters. Eventually CFB Esquimalt adjusted to the protesters, who insisted on their democratic right to gather and peacefully have their say. We were allowed to protest on Esquimalt Road, which is a public thoroughfare, but not on Admirals Road, which is on DND property. When we asked what would happen if we did trespass, we were told we would be arrested and handed over to the police, who later told us we'd simply be sent home. We didn't seem to be getting our point across.

So we made a banner that took six people to hold, reading: "Do We Want Nuclear Weapons In Our Harbour?" Loudmouths with their feet sticking out of the car window would yell, "Hell, yes. You're damned right we do."

Yet it seemed there was good reason to get upset about the dangers posed by the submarines because in 1986, DND began

Grannies took turns, six at a time, holding up this heavy banner outside the Canadian Forces Base in Esquimalt. Passing rowdies yelled, in response to the banner's question, "Hell, yes. You're damned right we do."

to brag about the effectiveness of its Nuclear Emergency Response Teams, known as NERTS, whose job it would be to fight a nuclear fire, evacuate the population, etc.

Some of the women in Extenuating Circumstances decided to become unofficial NERTS. We donned coveralls and hard hats and tied on daffodil-yellow armbands to give the appearance of officialdom. Then we set up a cardboard sign with a nuclear emblem on it and began to test the rain puddles. Bess had a battery-powered metronome, meant to scare crows out of her cherry trees, which we claimed would show the presence of low-level radiation. Joyce had a clipboard and a pencil to make notes on the frequency of those radioactive tick-tocks. The others scooped up rain from the puddles with spoons and turkey basters, poured the liquid back and forth in mayonnaise jars and made more notes, keeping very serious faces. We must have looked authentic, because many passersby engaged willingly in chit-chat about the nuclear danger out there. But when we moved to West Bay Marina, a beer-drinking yachtsman threatened to drown the lot of us in the sea.

There is always the small chance of a leak of radioactive material into the environment, though western navies say their nuclear-reactor safety principles and practices meet or exceed those adopted for the commercial nuclear-power industry. No maintenance on the reactor is allowed during a ship's stay in a Canadian port and no discharge of radioactive waste is permitted. The authorities insist that no release of radioactivity has ever been detected in a Canadian port and that the long-term environmental impact of these visits has been negligible.

If so, why is the base commander forbidden to leave the city when a nuclear-powered ship is in port? By the way, if you read the small print in your home-insurance policy you will see that you are not covered in the event of a nuclear explosion.

The nuclear disaster at Chernobyl had brought the danger of accidental radiation to public attention, all right, but maybe it was too threatening an issue for humorous treatment. We needed to do something different.

In October 1986, the women of Extenuating Circumstances got together with some University of Victoria students to dream up an action that would draw attention to the USS *Alaska*, a Trident-class submarine with the capability of launching ballistic missiles. It was about to pass Victoria on its way to its base in Bangor, Washington, where it would be fitted with 20 megatons of thermonuclear explosives — the force of 960 Hiroshimas and the ability to reach 192 separate cities. And Bangor, only 80 kilometres from Victoria, is home to 10 of those submarines.

Totally in line with our somewhat convoluted logic, we decided to protest the subs with pantyhose. After all, said Doran, pantyhose were symbols of subjugated women, and only men could have invented nuclear war. So she gathered up pantyhose donated by friends or purchased from the Salvation Army, the Goodwill store and the St. Vincent de Paul Society, and one afternoon at Bess's house we tied them all together and stretched them down her street to the length of two football fields — just about the length of a Trident submarine.

On Sunday, October 26, in the pouring rain, we stretched our pantyhose around the Ring Road of the University of Victoria, attaching to each crotch the name of a city in the Soviet Union that could be destroyed by one of the Trident submarines. It was a spectacular sight, but no media people came, perhaps because none of us knew then that the press don't take kindly to Sunday actions and don't want to read a five-page press release anyway. Only a few motorists rolled down their windows, stuck their heads out into the wind and rain and asked what on earth was going on. We gathered up the soaking, heavy hose and dumped them into Doran's car, where they got mouldy and eventually ended up in the garbage.

Undismayed, that very same evening, still in the wind and the rain, Doran persuaded us to take part in some spooky circle-dancing at Clover Point on Victoria's waterfront. It was supposed to put a curse on the USS *Alaska*, which nevertheless slipped past unscathed. Betty, who had gotten her feet wet leaping around in the grass at Clover Point, vowed never again to get involved with esoteric experiments and wannabe witches. There had to be a better way to protest and get public attention.

With the formation of the Raging Grannies, things would be different.

The first step to Granny-hood was dressing up. Off we went to the thrift stores, aiming primarily for hats: basic hats to decorate with whatever flowers, buttons, animals, birds and vegetables we could find. Feather boas were to come later and become a Victoria Granny trademark. The rest of the costume was up to individual choice. Betty's 1950s shocking-pink straw hat clashed wonderfully with her orange coat. Hilda emerged looking like a slightly dotty member of a Ruritanian royal family in a sky-blue, silver-embroidered bolero over a burgundy velvet gown adorned with bits of lace attached by large safety pins. Mary wore the pink dress she had made for her daughter's graduation, but added ostrich feathers and a butterfly. Joyce favoured romantic skirts. Bess kept her slacks on underneath her dress. Doran started out with a very respectable 1940s teal-blue coat with matching cloche hat, and then added bells. Fran went for sequins and boots.

Our very first action was on February 14, 1987, when we cornered MP Pat Crofton, chairman of the federal defence committee, and presented him with an Un-Valentine card to protest Canada's nuclear-arms policies. We had worked up some street theatre, huddling *en masse* under a very tattered "nuclear" umbrella while singing the very first Granny song, composed by Jane, with an original melody, no less. We sang, "Beneath the nuclear umbrella, we're as safe as we can be," inaugurating a tradition of satirical songs rather than preachy ditties. Pat Crofton did not seem impressed, nor did we get any press coverage.

Fran nobly invited us to make an appearance at the Pacifica Coffee House, frequented mostly by peace workers and friends. Half a dozen of us spoke up in turn about the dangers of nuclear ships visiting our ports. We got quite excited about uranium and prophetic about nuclear war. We were hitting our stride and the audience was captive, though strangely unresponsive. They settled farther down in their seats and stirred their coffee. Their eyes glazed over. The applause was tepidly polite and then there was a rush for more coffee. What a bore! We swore we would never do that again.

We'd profit from Jane's creative talents and concentrate on her satirical and provocative songs to get our message across — a tradition that has become more emblematic of the entire Granny movement than our hats or boas.

Jane composed a string of marvellous songs, including our introduction, which explained, "We're just a gaggle of Grannies, urging you off of your fannies." It was that song that inspired our collective nomenclature. Some women belong to clubs; we belong to gaggles. Jane wrote "Atomic Submarine" and "The Free Trade Trot," and songs in praise of bicycles and against dioxins. Some of

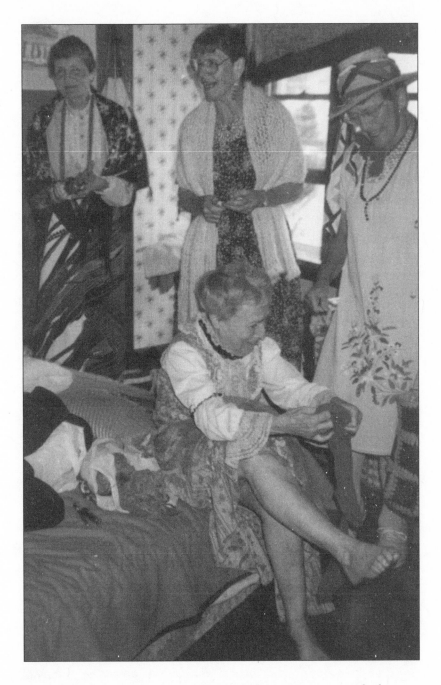

Joyce, Mary, Lois (left to right) and Hilda (sitting) get ready for a gig at an Unconvention.

This was our first action, outside MP Pat Crofton's office in February 1987. As Crofton was chairman of the national defence committee, we figured he was fair game. Left to right: Linda, Joyce, Jane, Bess, Betty, an identified supporter, Fran, Doran.

Although Crofton accepted our Un-Valentine protesting Canada's nuclear-arms policies, we sensed he was unimpressed. We did not get any press coverage.

her melodies were original; others were borrowed from well-known songs. She rehearsed us patiently, though our lack of musical talent was very obvious.

We were also nervous about being recognized in those days. Some were hoping our husbands or our neighbours wouldn't see us. At first, we were so reluctant to give out our real names to the press that we only agreed to be televised by our local cable-TV station in Bastion Square in downtown Victoria, at an event to promote the annual Victoria Peace Walk in April 1987, because they promised not to give our real names. Passersby thought we were hilarious. The film clip showed us singing and then zoomed in on one elderly gentleman holding his sides with laughter, unable to believe what he was seeing and hearing. But when a reporter for the Victoria *Times Colonist* wanted to take our picture and write an article on the condition that we gave our names, we said, "No thank you," and waltzed off.to a nearby restaurant for a cuppa, happy to remain anonymous and hoping our hats would disguise us.

Later on, Leslie Campbell, editor of the magazine *Focus on Women*, would explain, "The Grannies do not like to be identified by their real names, not because they fear retribution — most of them are bomb-proof — but because it's the group and its message that's important to them."[2]

We were so unsure of ourselves. We didn't want to be laughed at, not realizing then that looking totally ridiculous was to be our way of getting people to listen and think. We invented monikers like Granny Daffy Dilly, Granny Missile Free and Granny Shmanny, still clutching at anonymity. Such nervousness now seems ludicrous, since we have become so disgustingly proud of our odd appearance that we sashay downtown on the way to a gig in full feathers. We've even protested global warming in bikinis, though admittedly we wore tights underneath. But that was much later.

Gradually we became more courageous. We got so sure of ourselves that we allowed Fran to drag us to entertain the long Tuesday-night, half-price-movie lineups, where we had a captive audience. Betty announced, "If anybody throws money at me, I'm gone from this protesting business." But nobody did. Instead, we were told, kindly, "You must practise a lot to sing off key like that."

Nobody else seemed to notice us or our message until we got involved in an anti-uranium rally in February 1987 at the B.C. legislature. In its wisdom, the Social Credit government had lifted the moratorium on uranium mining in B.C., thereby opening up sites in the West Kootenays that had been closed to production since the 1970s because of environmental concerns. There had been startling reports of cancer among miners and their families at uranium mines in Saskatchewan, and alarm spread to B.C., with added fear about the possibility of radioactive particles leaking into nearby lakes and streams if the Kootenay mines opened up. Peace activists were upset about B.C. uranium ending up in American nuclear bombs, First Nations people living near the sites weren't happy about the threat, and labour unions didn't want any workers in unsafe conditions. So a giant protest was organized and the Raging Grannies were invited to take part, though how anyone knew we existed is still a mystery to us. We issued a press release with this opening zinger: "If you think news is entertainment, come and see the Raging Grannies at the legislature ..."

Jane whipped us into shape with her "Uranium Tango" to the tune of "Jealousy," and seven or eight of us huddled in a circle to gain courage, arms around each other like football players. This gave us a moment to remember why we were doing these crazy things, and a chance to straighten purple, yellow and blue flowered hats, pull on long white gloves, and snap shut our patent-leather purses.

"We could have taken up quilting," said Bess.

"Or bridge," said Joyce.

Betty said, "I'd sure like a drink."

"Later," said Fran. "We can do all that stuff after. We have to save the world first, before one of those 50,000 nuclear weapons out there goes off accidentally or on purpose."

So, knees knocking, we sang our song. We must have looked like bedraggled barnyard hens. We fiddled with our clothes. We forgot the words. Our singing was awful. But the brothers and sisters of the union movement applauded loudly. Then came our *tour de force*.

We announced we had a few briefs of our own to present to the legislature, and with stupendous aplomb we produced a laundry basket and a clothesline, which we stretched from one end of the stone steps to the other. Clothes pegs were unpacked, along with a selection of undies including long johns, boxers and bikinis, which we clipped onto the line. The crowd roared. Then we dumped our briefs back into the laundry basket and Granny-sprinted with it up the steps to the legislature doors, while Fran announced into the microphone that we intended to enter and present the briefs to the government, which was then in session. The legislative security guards would have none of it, blocking the doors solidly. But from the crowd massed on the lawn below came a chant of "Go, Grannies, go; go, Grannies, go ..." The security guards relented but made us leave our briefs behind.

Once inside we had no idea what to do. The guards and plain-clothes cops stared and we dissolved into giggles like schoolgirls who had successfully performed a daring prank. We didn't have the sense to push our advance and adjourned, instead, for tea and crumpets at the Royal BC Museum restaurant across the road.

A week or so later, a group of New Age mystics, calling themselves the Universal Peace Movement, set up tents on the lawn of the legislature, promising to stay until the moratorium on uranium mining was reinstated. When they weren't protesting, they ran a bead store in downtown Victoria. Was this a wonderful example of a co-operative community or was it a scam? While we were trying to decide, Premier Bill Vander Zalm solved our dilemma by turfing the tenters from "his" lawn. We went down to investigate, leaving our hats behind in case we were recognized. Very soon we ceased to be mere watchers as the battle began. Unarmed security guards were trying to pull down the tents, and a line of Black Maria vans drew up to cart the protesters away. Betty remembers hearing Hilda loudly exclaim, "Shame! Shame! Shame!" and seeing Joyce in the arms of a determined policeman.

Betty grabbed a TV cameraman and persuaded him to film the seizure of an innocent Granny. Of course, Joyce said she had merely held up a sign, but that evening's TV newscast showed her clobbering a security guard with a placard and she told us later she wasn't a bit sorry.

However, even Joyce was somewhat alarmed by later developments. The leader of the Universal Peace Movement ran off to India with the organization's money and somebody else's wife. He was later found decapitated by another member of the same "peaceful" sect. So much for peace.

Little did we know that one of the miscreants tugged out of those tents was Inger Kronseth, soon to become a Granny. She must have decided we were more desirable peace activists than her erstwhile companions, because she went to a Raging Granny performance soon afterward. She was telling a friend in the washroom about her desire to join us when she suddenly heard a voice piping up from one of the stalls, "Come to the next meeting."

Inger has the best credentials of all of us to be a Raging Granny. She had been part of the Danish resistance against the Nazis, inheriting the ardour of her maternal grandmother, who had been a fierce suffragette and had actually divorced her husband, which was unheard of before World War I. When Inger was nine, her mother died and her father married a woman whom Inger and her brother hated; they created their own campaign of silent disobedience and sabotage. When their stepmother offered her services to the German occupation force in 1940 and patriotic Danes painted a huge swastika on their front door, the children, now teenagers, turned their family feud into active resistance to the Nazis. Inger distributed illegal pamphlets and was taught how to use a gun, though she never fired a shot after a practice attempt that almost wounded a comrade. When she became too "hot" to stay in Denmark she escaped to Sweden in a fishboat. Her brother was killed, her father was arrested, and the young man she married was shot by a sniper six months after the wedding.

Inger came to Canada in 1956 after a career as a foreign correspondent in Europe. Her first job was cooking for a dude ranch. Then she married a miner and helped build a cabin in the B.C. Interior. In the back-to-the-land era, she tried homesteading, with a cow that refused to be milked, a tractor that wouldn't start and goats that ate the laundry. She also got started on environmental protesting by trying to stop the Armstrong Cheese Factory from throwing its waste into a nearby creek. This brought her to the tent protest on the lawn of the B.C. legislature and then to the Grannies. In 1993 she was one of the Clayoquot protesters sent to jail for blocking the bridge to the logging sites, and she would continue her environmental protests by trying to ban pesticide spraying and the development of a ski resort near her summer cabin in the Kootenays.

Inger is a tough trooper, with a personal history of great sadness — both of her husbands, her only daughter and her granddaughter were killed in separate accidents. But perhaps that is the source of her courage, which breathes new conviction into the more hesitant Grannies. Her humour also helps a lot: Inger is an experienced clown and a whiz at street theatre.

Following our debut at the anti-uranium rally, we went from nervousness to over-confidence. We signed up the following June to perform at the annual Seniors' Festival in Victoria's McPherson Theatre, sharing the stage with happy folk who square danced, yodelled and fiddled. We took the stage to a warm welcome; maybe they just liked our hats. However, as soon as the satirical nature of our songs became evident, the audience began to rustle and squirm.

Then came a song that referred to the Department of National Defence and the Royal Canadian Navy with a singular lack of respect. A man at the back yelled, "Go back to Russia, you pinkos!" Someone else shouted, "Shut up!" The booing began, some of it directed at us, some directed at our critics.

The only thing that saved us was Canadian patriotism. In our final song, Fran jumped up on cue to rip open her jacket and reveal the Canadian flag, to much applause. But downstairs in the dressing room that we shared with the polka people, the reception was somewhat frosty.

And so what! If we wanted to reach as wide an audience as possible, not just the committed, we'd have to brave a little booing. Fran recalls one service-club member at our gig at Norway House in Victoria turning his chair away from us and "mouthing off" to express his displeasure. But he didn't leave and nor did we, though one Granny remembers us retreating gradually farther backstage until, by the end, we seemed to be clinging to a piano against the back wall. Then there was the time at the White Eagle Hall when the audience got so loud that somebody called the cops and we sneaked out the back.

We tried singing to seniors in "daycare." They knew the tunes we used, but were totally unaware of what we were singing about. So we went for the younger generation and have had much more success with them, especially in songwriting workshops at primary schools. At high-school presentations, some teachers have turned us into a study subject, directing their charges to "listen carefully and then write a three-page essay." We have been stuck in corridors, singing at lunchtime to ravenous teens; our songs have been closely scrutinized by school principals in case we were too exciting.

On the other hand, we have had wonderful times helping kids to write their own songs on their own topics: homework, parents who don't understand, but also the environment and the homeless folk downtown.

Our favourite school, at Brentwood Bay near Victoria, has twice invited us for Earth Week. And those students are sharp. A grade eight student challenged us at question time, asking, "Did you all use cars to get here and talk about the environment?" Thank goodness we had carpooled.

We've been invited to many a university class, particularly classes in environmental science, sociology or women's studies. We've also tried our best with foreign students, who are here to learn English, with limited success. Satire is not easy to explain to Asian students. Nor is protesting, for that matter.

Nevertheless, the media were impressed. Patti Pitts of CHEK-TV (now CH) in Victoria interviewed Grannies at one of our meetings in 1987 and prefaced the interview by saying, "Their name suggests they're a rock group for the geriatric generation, but the Raging Grannies are much more than that. [They] shake a collective finger at those who pose a threat to world peace. They sing with humour

Back to school: Grannies Alison, Mary, Laura, Ruth, Betty, Fran (left to right) perform in 2000 at a middle school in Saanich, near Victoria.

so people listen. [At this year's Peace Walk] they were welcomed like a reigning rock group. Their rage is tempered with humour that cuts through nuclear phobias and generation gaps. The Raging Grannies have no plans to polish up their act, seek management or tamper with their grassroots image. When requested to perform, they will, without ever taking themselves too seriously."

In those early days, we were full of trust. When we joined others in the peace movement to protest the dangers of visiting nuclear warships at the annual Swiftsure yacht race, we put an empty cup for donations on the table. Doran had created a Granny gazebo with anti-nuclear signs. Bess, and her poodle, set up inside with leaflets and free coffee and was surprised to find so many visitors stuffing money into her donation cup. She was feeling so good she never noticed all the money disappearing with one of our co-organizers.

We had a lot to learn.

Sometimes we bombed. Sometimes we got raves, but that didn't always mean we got noticed in the press. In 1988 we sang to a Vancouver crowd estimated at 100,000 people taking part in Canada's largest peace walk ever. We were called back for an encore. Unfortunately, the roof of a new supermarket fell in that afternoon, so none of the video footage taken of us found room on the local TV news.

But we were buoyed by an article in Air Canada's *enRoute* magazine in April 1989, by one of our favourite writers. West-coast novelist Audrey Thomas was profiling Victoria and included its Raging Grannies: "Some of Victoria's seniors, like the Raging Grannies, don't take retirement sitting down. They are often found at the stolid Parliament Buildings, protesting against nuclear submarines ... The closest Victoria comes to a terrorist group is the Raging Grannies — a group of women who sing and present skits and generally indulge in peaceful issues and highly political protests aimed at the U.S. Navy submarines that ply the up-island waters."[3] We loved the soft-focus, sepia-toned picture that Mary Ellen McQuaig took to go with the article.

Not surprisingly, that article brought lots of requests to sing. One of the first was from Blairmore, Alberta. They wanted us to sing for a women's group in June 1989. Already, other Granny groups were starting to form, with Gabriola Island, Salt Spring Island and then Vancouver joining us within a year. But there was no network of Granny gaggles across the country as there is today, so the Victoria gaggle was "it." That is why we embarked on a series of road adventures that tested our tolerance and our bank balances, and still makes us laugh today.

With only two cars for nine Grannies, plus our hats, costumes and emergency food supplies, we should have anticipated disaster. It didn't help that we were all stuffed inside warm coats because we knew it always snowed in the Rockies, even in June. Naturally, we were driving into a heat wave.

Packed into one of the cars was a new Granny, Anne Pask. Tiny but tough, Anne became our conscience. She was deeply religious; she'd even presided over church services as part of her regular visits to William Head, the local federal penitentiary. But Anne was also very practical and a lover of fun. A nurse for more than 40 years, most of them served in the Arctic, she once survived a plane crash that trapped her in frigid water up to her mouth, trying to save the patient she was escorting south. Her idea of retirement in 1983 was a peace pilgrimage to Jerusalem and then a tour of duty as nurse aboard Greenpeace's *Pacific Peacemaker*, sailing close to the Marshall Islands' atomic-bomb test site. While others protested the visits of nuclear submarines to Nanoose by writing letters, Anne walked more than 120 kilometres from Victoria to Nanoose, alone, but with garden tools in her pack so that she could work in return for hospitality on her way.

"The police stopped and asked me if I was all right, so I had a chance to tell them why I was walking to Nanoose and what should be done about those nuclear vessels," says Anne.

We never fully appreciated Anne's many charms until the day we were invited to Merve Wilkinson's woodlot at Yellow Point, north of Victoria. Wildwood has now become a shrine for environmentalists, and Merve, the guru at that shrine, is venerated by students and tree huggers from all around the world. But we didn't realize that he was also a man with an eye for a woman. Anne was chosen to write and thank him for our visit; instead, we learned later, she drove up and took him home-baked cookies. And that was the start of the romance that led to Anne's first marriage.

She had once seriously considered marriage and even had her wedding gown made, but changed her mind. In April 1992, 37 years later, she walked down the aisle in that same white-and- gold, ballerina-length dress that still fit. Grannies from Victoria, Salt Spring Island, Gabriola Island and Vancouver formed an arch of Granny umbrellas as the newlyweds left the church. We were thrilled but sad, because it meant Anne would no longer have time for us, becoming the companion of a man who was to be recognized as one of B.C.'s most eminent authorities on sustainable forestry and eventually become a member of the Order of Canada. But while she stayed with our gaggle, Anne was a guiding light.

"You never know what can happen when you pass the word along," says Anne.

The plan for our Blairmore trip — Anne's bright idea — was for the two cars to rendezvous near the entrance to the Hope–Princeton highway at a vaguely remembered restaurant. Not only did we fail to find each other, we failed to find the right highway. When the passengers in the Volvo at last spotted the Toyota, it was pouring forth black smoke. Two kindly motorists promised to send a tow truck, but when they admitted they were nuclear physicists, they were treated to an anti-nuclear earful and given Granny calling cards for their pains. They left us sitting in a circle on a patch of grass like elderly flower children, hoping for rescue.

Inger tried to speak German to the German garage owner, who promised to get a new clutch from Vancouver and have it installed some time the next day. A motel allowed eight of us to sleep for $30, two to a bed in three beds and two on the floor, while Inger wisely opted to sleep in her Volvo and avoid many arguments about who was snoring and how wide open the window should be. We spent the next day repacking our clothes to ease the load on the fragile Toyota, whose new clutch cost nearly $500. Thank goodness for VISA.

By now we were learning who were the dawdlers, who would get lost and who wanted to be boss. It didn't help to have so many former teachers among us. When we got tired of the road or were held up by road repairs, we'd get out and try Tai Chi or rehearse our Granny songs. Other drivers seemed nonplussed rather than appreciative. As the scenery got greener, the environmentalists among us got out to finger the moss. The hotter it got, the slower we got, until we exploded from the cars in Osoyoos, some in swimsuits, some in underwear, to plunge into a cold lake, discovering later that it was famous for its pollution from the pesticides used to spray local orchards.

More time was wasted searching for ice cream and antiques before we arrived at our first gig in Greenwood, by which time we were so tired and cranky that one of us had a temper tantrum and the rest of us sulked. A group hug got us reconciled enough to sing at the United Church to kind applause. Betty got into the rye that night and felt awful the next morning, even though the sky was forget-me-not blue and we'd bought enough food for a typical Granny picnic — canned salmon, sardines, pineapple, tomatoes, celery, lettuce, hard-boiled eggs, yogurt, cheese, dark bread and homemade cake. Yes, we do love food.

We did eventually get to Blairmore to sing, and we did learn from this first long-distance performance that Grannies can't be rushed and need to take time out for some fun.

Two months later we took to the road again, to sing at the Edmonton Fringe Festival. It was one of our finest appearances. This is how the *Edmonton Journal* recorded it: "When the Victoria Grannies roll across the stage, holding decidedly phallic versions of MX missiles while singing the old air force ditty, 'Roll Me Over,' even the most loquacious politician is reduced to aghast silence."[4]

To us, however, our performance was the ultimate statement on how the arms race and the trillion-dollar military-industrial complex had screwed up the world. It was also our ultimate feminist, non-intellectual, anti-war statement.

If the medium is the message, in rolling around on that stage in Edmonton in the August sun we were, like Stanley Kubrick's 1963 film *Dr. Strangelove,* linking two of the basic male instincts — sex drive and the urge to kill. We were also showing how, in the male mind, an exploding guided missile mimics the sexual bang felt at the moment of ejaculation.

While deciding on this parody we were influenced by Doran, who brought up Dr. Helen Caldicott's concept of missile envy. That got Betty remembering how she naively used to join in singing the World War II song "Roll Me Over" at the culmination of parties in the air force officers' mess. So, here's how our bombshell went. No surprise that Grannies Anne, Joyce and Inger refused to take part, but they did stand on the sidelines and bellow out the chorus:

This is number one
And the fun has just begun
Roll me over
Lay me down
And do it again

Roll me over
In the clover
Roll me over
Lay me down
And do it again

This is number two
And the rest is up to you
Etc.

We lined up across the stage and one by one stepped forward to sing solo, holding up a clearly labelled missile. After singing her bit each Granny lay down on the stage, feet to the audience, and held the handmade missile/penis over her body: Doran, Tomahawk cruise missile; Fran, Terrier missile; Lois, Harpoon missile (this was the most recognizably phallic symbol of all: it was fat, about three feet long, covered with aluminum foil, and had a shiny red tip); Kathy, Peacekeeper missile; Betty, MX missile (10 feet long, made from cardboard carpet tubes); Hilda, Trident I missile (when she lay down she lost both her hat and her wig — we were getting very hysterical at this point); Linda, Trident II missile (there were red, white and blue ribbons flying from this one. We're not sure Linda had the message right, since her choice of words was: "This is number seven and now I'm up in heaven."). We hoped her conclusion was lost in the noisy enthusiasm from the audience.

We rolled about, getting more and more giggly and slightly hysterical as the chorus, by now being roared by the Fringe audience too, flowed over us. This was the last act of the afternoon and our first and only performance at the Edmonton Fringe Festival. We performed it once more at a women's conference. They weren't impressed. We never did it again.

The Salt Spring Grannies were scheduled to perform the next day at the Fringe. After the report in the *Edmonton Journal* about those naughty Grannies from Victoria, they were thrilled with the huge audience. However, their gig was quite staid, and the audience certainly wasn't treated to our sort of impropriety.

We're still amazed we weren't run out of town. After our outrageous performance we chilled out by taking a dip in the West Edmonton Mall's surf pool. Fran had wangled us a reduced entry fee as a family.

Indeed, we do tend to behave like a somewhat dysfunctional family when we're on the road. We argue in cars and more than one driver has slammed on the brakes, announcing — just as we did as parents — that she wouldn't drive another inch unless everybody shut up. It's worse when we take dogs along, as our gaggle includes fanatical dog lovers and dog haters. We did once manage to leave Joyce behind at a gas station on the way to a

First Nations conference near Tofino, on Vancouver Island's west coast. But we remembered her five kilometres later, went back and apologized. We're not very good at ferries. We get in the wrong lineup and make everybody back out. We even lose our way aboard ferries. Two Grannies who got lost on the ferry to Horseshoe Bay near Vancouver were devastated to hear a public announcement requesting "two elderly ladies" to report to the crew, who would help them find the way to the right car deck.

Those early trips to gigs frayed but tempered us, as we lost and found each other and located the washrooms in time. It also put us off any aspirations to the life of an entertainer. Yes, we were having fun, but it was all so exhausting. We had a message to deliver and we had to find different ways to deliver it, besides entertaining a sympathetic audience. And we had to zero in on our primary goal — world peace.

OH DEAR WHAT CAN THE MATTER BE?

Sung to the tune of "Oh Dear What Can the Matter Be?" traditional; lyrics by Alison Acker

Oh Dear, what can the matter be?
We've been attacked by the forces of gravity.
Fat has appeared where there once was concavity.
Nobody said life was fair.

Older men become more adorable
Even though their figure's deplorable.
Their physique is always insurable
With or without their gray hair.

Older women are thought unattractive,
They're shunned as if they were radioactive.
They jiggle so when they become active.
It's back to that old rocking chair.

Well, these gray mares, we ain't what we used to be.
We've given up on respectability.
Don't give a fig for acceptability
We're far too AWESOME to care.

ALL AT SEA

As we grow older we should
become not less radical but more so.
— *Margaret Laurence*

Right from the start, those pesky visiting nuclear submarines had been our primary target. We decided to go after them where they lived — in the ocean. The arrival of the USS *Indianapolis* in 1987 gave us our first opportunity. We were going to chase another of those "Chernobyls in tin cans" away from our harbour. We knew it was there because Betty had her telescope handy at the window of her Esquimalt home, and we knew it was bad because we had studied *Jane's Fighting Ships*, which had been presented to the Esquimalt library by a departing Canadian admiral. He probably never guessed who would be using it most. This was before the naval base was required by law to give out the name or hull number of any visiting foreign warship — a great help in future actions after we had set up a system of regularly badgering the base's public affairs officer.

Our prey having been sighted, Doran and Betty scrambled a gaggle of Grannies together and cajoled a reluctant CHEK-TV cameraman into joining us at the Esquimalt First Nations Reserve adjacent to the base. Doran rented a rowboat from a family on the reserve. Fran brought her canoe, tenuously tied on top of her car with string. Doran rowed the boat, accompanied by Betty and the cameraman. Fran and Mary paddled the canoe, with Bess lolling in the middle wearing a diaphanous, lemon-yellow hat with silk ribbons. She was somewhat protected from the sun by our nuclear umbrella full of holes. She let her fingers run through the water, for all the world as if she were on her leisurely way to a picnic.

The cameraman took pictures of the dull, dense, black sub, looking pretty benign as it sat low in the water behind a row of bright yellow floats. Doran kept up a running commentary and

As Bess lolls under the "nuclear umbrella," Fran and Mary paddle Fran's canoe toward the USS submarine Indianapolis at the Esquimalt naval base in 1987.

the Grannies in the other boat tried to sing above it. We're not sure how much of our message the sailors heard, but they did invite us to tea — at least, that is what we think they said. We tossed bunches of flowers as close to the sub as we could, which wasn't very close because a military police Zodiac buzzed out to tell us that if we so much as touched the yellow boom around the submarine we would all be arrested. The camera caught a pride of senior naval officers in glittering gold braid standing dockside and the blue flashing lights on military police cars in the background. We decided it was time to head for shore.

That was only the first of many times we went out in kayaks, canoes or rowboats, dressed in full Granny gear. Betty once agreed to try out an experimental kayak because you could paddle it lying down; she had not anticipated that this would mean showing her knickers.

Despite losing dignity, we've gathered a great deal of press coverage for our naval forays. That first launching was the lead story on the TV news that evening, and it did carry our message about nuclear dangers. If we had to get a little wet to get people's attention, so be it.

We also wanted to get our facts right. We needed to know more about the threat posed to the entire Pacific area by those Trident submarines that were gliding up and down the coast and who knows where else. What were other people doing about it? The next month four Grannies travelled to Ground Zero, a peace camp set up outside the submarine base at Bangor, Washington. The base holds the third-largest stockpile of nuclear weapons in the United States. We were highly impressed by the ongoing campaign of civil disobedience waged by a group of American peace activists, and watched with respect as they knelt in front of the American flag in the military compound before being hauled away on a charge of trespassing. Despite many years of protesting, not one of them has ever been convicted.

By now Kathy Hall had joined us. She had met Fran when they were both training as counsellors in Victoria. Like Fran, she was

A view from Betty's house: Ships, including a sub in the foreground, gather off Victoria in 1985 in celebration of the 75th anniversary of the Royal Canadian Navy.

an American. Born into an Irish-Catholic family in Philadelphia, she was getting into trouble right from the age of four when she was caught playing with the neighbourhood Black kids. She had a hard time reconciling the very flag-waving, patriotic views of her father with the rebel songs he used to sing about the 1916 uprising in Ireland. After working in a children's shelter and then as a counsellor in a U.S. ghetto, she got caught up in the Vietnam war protests, encouraged her husband to set fire to his draft card and moved with him and their two sons to Salt Spring Island, where they raised vegetables and started an independent school.

When she joined the Grannies, Kathy was juggling part-time jobs as teacher, counsellor and relief housekeeper, and her marriage was coming apart. She soon made a strong friendship with Doran and was later to join her on a farm in the Cowichan Valley.

Doran, Lois and four local protesters experienced arrest a year later. They were detained in August 1988, after stepping onto the dock of Winchelsea Island, which is Department of National Defence territory off the Nanoose weapons-testing site north of Nanaimo. But the embarrassed cop who arrested them said he didn't really want to jail Grannies, and the trespassing charges were never pursued.

We weren't anxious to get arrested, but we did want our cause made public. And we really had a chance in 1990, when the CBC-TV series *Man Alive* called with plans to feature us in a program. Fortuitously, Greenpeace was about to stage an action against those nuclear ships in Esquimalt Harbour, and we were also on the point of hosting the third Unconvention of Raging Grannies. What an opportunity.

David Cherniack, the producer, came to our potluck lunch, which consisted of more bread than cheese until Doran scurried out to buy more cheddar. We arranged for the TV crew to go aboard the Greenpeace ship *Rainbow Warrior II* along with the Grannies the next day, when two brave members of Greenpeace would hang a large anti-nuclear banner from a crane in Esquimalt Harbour, practically under the eyes of the military police. The cameraman focused on our feet as we tramped in our pink running shoes down the dock and onto the *Rainbow Warrior II*. And he kept shooting as we sang aboard the boat and cheered the Greenpeace climbers, thanking God we weren't expected to do anything so athletic. (When they appeared in court we were there to support them, in our hats, and they got off with a conditional discharge.)

After the arrest, the *Man Alive* crew followed us to the perimeter of the base, where Doran and Kathy teased the security guards. They both clambered up the chain-link fence with a banner, threw over their hats and threatened to jump after them, until the hats were duly retrieved by one of the guards. As we were leaving, the cameraman filmed Fran's polite but forceful conversation with a

Inger (left) and Lois aboard the Rainbow Warrior II *in Esquimalt Harbour.*

base worker in her car, who yelled her outrage and asked how we would like it if Saddam Hussein came to Canada and took our cars away! We didn't think it very likely.

Then we all adjourned to the Granny Unconvention. These get-togethers had begun in 1988, when the Salt Spring gaggle invited us over for a visit of song sharing and strategy. The next year was Gabriola Island's turn, and now it was ours. We hosted the other B.C. Grannies at Glenairley, a retreat centre west of Victoria, which belonged to the Sisters of St. Ann. The CBC cameraman put crabapples in our beds and David Cherniack's lengthy interviews took over much of the proceedings.

Anne gave a wonderful interview recalling her nights at sea on the *Pacific Peacemaker*, days away from land, watching the stars. Other Grannies rhapsodized about the patience of spiders. The result was a great program, heavy on spirituality, with the addition of some circle-dancing (not by us, but *Man Alive* was supposed to have a spiritual focus, so who were we to object?). The scenic shots of Victoria and lots of wet trees made a marvellous backdrop. Grannies from the other gaggles attending the Unconvention didn't seem to mind being involved in a CBC program, though we should have warned them ahead of time about the TV crew and the tampered beds.

We often had arguments about how much we should co-operate with Greenpeace, as we were jealous of our own identity. Doran once accused those of us who were Greenpeace devotees of being "like Catholics kow-towing to the pope." But that didn't stop her joining a group of us aboard the *Rainbow Warrior II* when it sailed from Prince Rupert to Ketchikan, Alaska, to protest the use of Dixon Entrance by U.S. nuclear vessels. We're dogged defenders of Canadian sovereignty and that was our territory, not open water. In pouring rain, Doran and Kathy jumped from a Greenpeace Zodiac onto Back Island, which constituted the U.S. Navy base. No military was present, but Doran and Kathy sang their anti-nuke songs anyway. Later we did meet local activists and First Nations people to discuss the whittling away of Canadian sovereignty.

We shifted our focus back to Victoria. We managed to climb aboard an antique red-and-yellow fire engine with a large bell and an even larger sound system so that we could take part in the annual Oak Bay Tea Party parade and bellow forth at the tweedy set lining the streets. That was the last time we were invited. In January 1990 we invaded the very stately New Year's Day levee at Government House in full costume. We did try to behave among Victoria's worthiest citizens, but when the band started playing we couldn't help but dance. Jim Gibson reported in the *Times Colonist* that the crowd "stood transfixed but perhaps was too busy juggling teacups and neat little nibbles to applaud the anti-nuclear nannas. Then again, it might have been appalled — not amused — by the intrusion of street theatre at the most staid of events."

At the next year's levee, when the Gulf War seemed about to begin, we were attired in black from top to toe and explained to the lieutenant-governor why we were draped in mourning for those who would suffer in the war. He seemed a little fazed but was, of course, polite.

Searching for another angle, we decided to launch our very own navy and to do it in Ottawa. We registered our fleet officially under the Societies Act as "The Raging Granny Anti-Nuclear Armada," not being allowed to register as a navy because, we were told, "only nation states can have navies." And it just so happened that in April 1990, we were invited to sing at a federal-provincial government-funded conference called "Aging into the Twenty-first Century" to be held in Ottawa.

Perhaps the conveners thought of us as role models, that being a Raging Granny would hold back the effects of time or at least be a healthy way to travel toward the inevitable. Who cared? We were delighted at being paid to go to Ottawa because it would be a marvellous opportunity to introduce our navy to the feds. It would also give us a great chance to ambush federal politicians with our message. The honorarium was for eight Grannies. Nobody wanted to be left behind, so 13 of us went and shared the money around, sleeping cheap with extra cots, Granny style.

We sent Anne Pask ahead to Ottawa to get us an appointment with someone from the Department of National Defence, to contact the media and organize our prop — one very small inflatable boat to represent our navy. It would be a symbolic baptism. It took three taxis to get us and our already-inflated boat to the CBC studio in Ottawa to explain our exploits on Peter Gzowski's *Morningside*, and then on to Parliament Hill. We plopped our boat into the Peace Fountain and the two smallest grannies, Anne and Hilda, climbed in with paddles. A kindly police officer voiced his concern that

Anne and Hilda might be overcome by fumes from the Centennial Flame, but they kept paddling. When he insisted, they moved to the concrete surrounding the pool.

The Ottawa media loved us: "Only from the land of the lotus-eaters would 13 Raging Grannies sally forth to Parliament Hill to launch their own toy navy. That there was hardly enough

We launch our navy on Parliament Hill in April 1990 (the flagship was an inflatable boat that we popped into the Peace Fountain). Left to right: Alison, Bess, Joyce, Lois, Doran. Front: Anne Pask.

water in the moat around the Centennial Flame to float a rubber ducky didn't deter them in the least. They rowed their boat on the concrete shoulder," said the *Ottawa Citizen*.

Besides getting great coverage for our anti-nuclear campaign, we fulfilled our obligations to the conference. We had several gigs and conducted songwriting workshops to empower seniors; many were fed up with being patronized by the caregiving bureaucracy, which tends to pat seniors on the head and ignore them.

Then we got a chance to tackle Department of National Defence officials about Canada's willingness to host nuclear-armed American vessels. We went into the House of Commons and reluctantly surrendered our hats to security guards at the door. Ushered into a very plush meeting room and invited to take our seats way down a long table, we plumped instead for the big chairs with the arms and did our best to take over from the four male ministry officials who talked down to us and didn't want to listen. We also sang at Prime Minister Brian Mulroney before he could duck into his limo and head for home, and chatted in their offices with the few friendly New Democratic Party MPs who shared our concern.

Back in Victoria, now that our navy was launched nationally and our armada registered as a non-profit society, we thought perhaps we could raise money to buy our own boat. One kayak kept springing a leak and Fran's canoe was heavy. Nevertheless they had to do when we joined 56 other boats in Victoria Harbour to observe United Nations Disarmament Week in 1990. We considered buying a Zodiac, tried one out and scared ourselves silly, bucking over the waves with a roar. Besides, the Zodiac was an environmental disaster: noisy and heavy on gas.

Lo and behold, in April 1991 a retired Canadian warship was put up for tender, for demolition or purchase. We put in a notice of interest, which would allow us to inspect the boat. Finding our way to HMCS *Chaudiere*, moored "somewhere" off Colwood, was not easy. Nor was our embarkation. We were permitted to go aboard only because we had replied to a War Assets advertisement, so the navy had to consider us legitimate. We brought along a hammer, to test for telltale bulges in the sides, but had to surrender it to the authorities. Unfortunately, the *Chaudiere* just wouldn't do. "Stripped, Worn Warship Too Messy for Grannies," trumpeted the *Times Colonist*: "The Raging Grannies found it 'too messy,' so they wouldn't adopt it for their navy. 'We found it needed a tremendous amount of house-cleaning … it was covered with a lot of bird

This is the Zodiac that we (briefly) thought that we could a) afford and b) run. We scared ourselves silly on our test run.

dirt and rat dirt and would need an awful lot of scrubbing … We thought we might make a down payment but decided it was too messy for us.'"

We managed the best we could with our old boats, hampered by the U.S. Navy's refusal to give advance notice of its ships' movements. Betty thought her way around that. She knew that the Victoria Chamber of Commerce loved those navy visits and the cash they generated, so when a visit by an aircraft carrier was announced she phoned up and was given another number to call.

"Can you tell me what time the American sailors are coming to Victoria?" Betty lisped seductively.

"Sorry," was the cultured reply from a businesswoman. "That is top-secret information. Why do you want to know? Where did you get this phone number?"

"We ... er ... um ..." Betty didn't want to tell a lie. "I got your phone number from the chamber and it's like this, ma'am. My girls want to meet the sailors."

"Oh, but of course. Yes, I do understand. Have your girls dock-side at Ogden Point around 11 in the morning. There'll be lots and lots of sailors for them. And listen, the usual bars will be offering a free first drink. Have a great time."

Betty's other self-imposed responsibility with Granny protests was to alert the port authorities about any upcoming peaceful demonstration so that nervous Nellies on a warship would not be too surprised. In one case, she forgot until two hours before the event. She phoned the Canadian Coast Guard and the Victoria harbourmaster to tell them about an imminent protest and the ship's visit to shore was cancelled within the hour. (She understands that her friends, who had really wanted to protest, were not too pleased with her action, but our aim was achieved. We had indeed spooked the U.S. Navy and chased their ship away.)

But they came back. In October 1991, the USS *Shasta*, an ammunition ship capable of transporting nuclear weapons, had the cheek to dock right at Ogden Point in downtown Victoria. Joyce, Fran and Betty drove down, along with a new recruit, Alison Acker. We found a Canadian navy lieutenant on duty and sent him with a note to the U.S. commander to ask if there were nukes on board.

When he failed to return, we marched smartly past some security guards. An apoplectic security guard flew out of his office and ordered us to retreat. We refused, although the *Times Colonist* photographer following us decided to fall back. Then a Canadian Coast Guard official demanded identification. The others stalled while Alison returned to the car to find her driver's licence. A Canadian officer and his American colleague arrived, but refused to discuss nuclear weapons on the dock with us. Any discussion would have to take place outside the security gate, where little old lady civilians were more or less tolerated. We argued this point of view with them, but they were adamant. We presumed it meant that although the American ship was tied up at a Canadian dock, the Americans made the rules of engagement. We sovereignists were upset. We were also put off by the American emissary telling us his captain had docked because he so dearly wanted to see Victoria. All right for the Chamber of Commerce, but not for Grannies. The *Times Colonist* headlined the story: "A Pleasant Visit But No Answers for Grannies."

On another occasion, the USS *Greenville* glided into the Esquimalt base with Santa Claus on its conning tower. An obliging young lawyer drew up a writ for us, charging the sub's captain with

One of Victoria's finest checks out Fran (left) and Betty. We were at Ogden Point in Victoria, protesting the presence of the USS aircraft carrier Abraham Lincoln. *The Grannies have been known to use some interesting tactics to find out when ships like this come into port.*

defaming the good name of Santa Claus. When we "Female Friends of Santa" tried to deliver it, we were thwarted by the military police. But Betty, after a lifetime with a military husband, knew her rights and demanded to see the duty officer, who listened politely and assured us he would get the writ to his captain, but that was as far as we could get. We even tried the washroom ploy, insisting on our right to use the facilities, which we knew were far beyond the gate. No sympathy at all. Maybe it was our clothes. Maybe we shouldn't always look like Grannies. We might do better in disguise.

We had already tried a different costume in order to infiltrate the Conservative ranks. In 1989, when Progressive Conservative Minister of Trade Pat Carney was scheduled to speak at the Empress Hotel under the auspices of the local Chamber of Commerce, pushing NAFTA and free trade, we dug out pleated skirts, cashmere sweaters and pearls in order to blend in with the ambience of this elegant hotel and the expected audience of Conservatives. Six of us lined up among groups of the party faithful. We must have looked the part. We cornered Pat Carney in the hotel lobby and, yes, she would love to hear Jane's "Free Trade Trot." It started out as a hymn of praise for free trade, but soon segued into satire:

> We may not know where our next job's coming from,
> But we'll have Calvin Klein on all our bum-bum,
> bumpty bum-bums.

The look of joy vanished from Pat Carney's face. Her eyes flashed fire, but she stuck it out and listened to the end.

"Culture isn't part of the package. Your singing is better than your logic," she pronounced. And, all sails set, she stormed into the banquet room.

We tried to catch her eye another time when a reception was laid on for her and other feds at Government House. We couldn't get inside the gates so we laid on our own reception just outside — a tea party, with a tea wagon on wheels, a silver tea service and even biscuits. This time our concern was those nuclear ships, and we shouted and rattled our teacups at each chauffeured limousine, getting waves, stares, smiles and grimaces, but no media attention; the security men had detoured the media bus to the second gate at Government House. Two of us were allowed in to try and inveigle some media interest and a couple of jaded-looking reporters did come out to ask us questions, but we got no coverage.

Maybe we should try another form of attire. We tried to get the attention of Minister of Defence Perrin Beatty when he came to Victoria in 1988 by wearing deep-mourning veils, but he sprinted past us to an interview with CFAX radio.

We got closer to Bill McKnight, who followed Beatty in the job, donning golf togs when he came to open a new golf course and speak to yet another Chamber of Commerce meeting. Linda presented him with a golf ball inscribed with the peace symbol but he refused to take it. He began his pep talk by saying that after meeting the Raging Grannies he thought the golf club should increase its fees to keep us out.

We were hoping for better things with Mary Collins, the associate minister of defence, who came to speak at the University of Victoria in 1989. We trundled out there only to find the meeting cancelled, so we pinned a note to the door suggesting, half humorously, that the threat of the Granny presence must have scuttled the meeting altogether.

An unsigned letter appeared in the UVic student paper *The Martlet*: "To the Raging Grannies: You flatter yourself by assuming your presence forced the cancellation. It's nice to see that people of your generation have finally raised your consciousness about today's issues. Unfortunately, your enlightenment has come years too late."[1]

There was a reply in the next issue: "Granny-bashing is dead wrong. The level of bad assumptions and pettiness was so high in your letter ... what would you have them do? Would you have them consigned to a retirement home to sit around and complain about the high price of tea?"[2]

Quite encouraged, we planned another attack on Mary Collins, who was booked for an electronics trade fair. Since electronics have a military application and we did not like the idea of B.C. firms angling for contracts to perpetuate the Cold War — the Berlin Wall had fallen only days before — we wanted to make it quite clear we would not tolerate even the *thought* of Victoria hosting an arms trade show.

We gussied ourselves up with lots of gold braid. Doran and Kathy, as generals from some operetta, wore Goodwill army jackets with green and pink plastic streamers in lieu of campaign ribbons. Betty left the price tag stapled to the sleeve of a chief warrant officer's greatcoat that she was able to return to the Value Village thrift store the next day. Her RCAF pilot's flying cap, with ostrich feathers that tickled, enhanced the effect. Joyce opted for her white plastic Nuclear Emergency Response Team coveralls and a surgical mask.

Watched over by a Mulroney mask fashioned by Bess and Mary, Grannies Joyce, Jean McLaren, Fran, Doran, Mary, Betty, Linda, Lois and Anne Pask (left to right) protest the arms trade at the Victoria Conference Centre in 1989.

We managed to get inside the Victoria Conference Centre and gradually insinuated ourselves up the stairs toward the banquet room. We were met by a wall of plain-clothed security people, in good humour but adamant that we proceed no farther. Betty pulled out a Raging Granny calling card and, in her best writing, asked for a meeting with the honourable lady minister. A grinning military person returned with the answer, "Declining at the moment, but perhaps at another, more convenient time?" So we decided to sing our "London Bridge" song, forming a bridge and ducking under linked arms as we sang, "The Berlin Wall is falling down ... Our dear Mary O."

At this, the TV cameras turned away from Terry Wolfwood, spokesperson for the Canadian Voice of Women for Peace, who was giving her opinions of the trade show, and pointed at us. Doran aimed right at the camera with her own views: "Grannies have dedicated the morning to spitting and polishing our buttons and adorning our persons in finery in confident expectation of conferring with the associate minister of national defence about women's forebodings about war." And that's what got on TV: our rant, not Terry's. We did write Terry an apology later, but relations have been somewhat frosty ever since.

Mary Collins's TV spot showed her announcing a brand-spanking-new reserve officers' mess and saying nothing about war, but we have to admit that her appearance, with perfectly coiffed, tawny-golden hair, peaches-and-cream complexion and Marilyn Monroe voice, was more pleasing than the Grannies'.

Well, one politician did like us, so there. In 1989 the Right Honourable Joe Clark, then Minister of Foreign Affairs in Brian Mulroney's cabinet, came to Victoria to speak to still yet another Chamber of Commerce meeting. We hung out at the entrance to the Princess Mary Restaurant, half of which is a boat on dry land. Security decided we were harmless, and when Clark arrived on the scene we were dazzled to hear him say, "At last I get to meet the Raging Grannies." The evening news showed him unfazed by a white-gloved Granny shaking a finger at him for allowing nuclear warships into Canada. Edited out was Linda tickling him under his chin with her flaming-red feather boa.

Round about this time we lost our songwriter, Jane Mackey, who went back to full-time work and didn't have time for Grannying. Besides, she was getting frustrated with trying to coach the tone-deaf. By luck, another songwriter came to the rescue. Alison Acker had been living in Toronto when she heard about the Victoria Grannies from a friend. She was already considering moving to Victoria on her retirement; the chance of becoming a Raging Granny convinced her. She turned up at one of our gigs a month after arriving in 1989, and got invited to a meeting. When she offered to write songs, she was promptly added.

Alison seemed like good material, since she had been thrown out of the University of Nottingham in England at the age of 17. Workers at Boots drugstores were on strike, so, because Jesse Boot was the founder of her university, she helped paint his statue with bright red paint, which may not have helped the strikers but sure got attention. Somehow she managed to pursue a respectable career as a journalist in England and then as a university professor in Canada and wrote two books, *Children of the Volcano* and *Honduras: The Making of a Banana Republic*. She also had two short but sweet marriages (both husbands died) and a lengthy affair with a renowned Canadian poet. He immortalized her toes and other attributes in his poetry. She took those toes to Latin America, working for human rights and justice, first for the Chileans and then for Central Americans. She would raise money for the Salvadoran guerrillas and fly south with it stuffed in her bra, praying that no one would search her. She wrote many articles and protested Canada's *laissez-faire* stand on atrocities down south. She was protesting our foreign policy in Ottawa when she collected two criminal convictions (for mischief) and learned the power of challenging authority in a public but peaceful way. "Sitting in the middle of the road watching cars drive up to your feet and then stop got me hooked," she confesses. Yes, there was something an ordinary person could do besides writing letters to MPs and voting.

When Alison moved to Victoria, she bought a condominium on Portage Inlet, with the misguided idea of kayaking to buy her groceries in town. But both the condo and the kayak developed leaks and Alison moved closer to downtown, into a condo designed by a compatriot, Francis Rattenbury. All the other Grannies say that Alison lives her life too fast. She gets impatient at meetings and nags everybody into actions. But since she makes most of the banners and is always there to hold them up, and writes most of the songs, we put up with her.

Soon after Alison arrived, there was a fundraising party to buy more boats for the Granny navy. It was held at Doran's home in an affluent area of Victoria, but was not quite what the neighbours would expect. Shreds of gaudy, sparkly Christmas decorations dripped from the rhododendrons and roses.

Where did Doran get the piles of outdated *Manchester Guardians*, broken pottery camels, torn lace tablecloths, faded striped bedsheets and lonely unmatched, chipped china, all offered for sale? We knew she was creative, but maybe this was a political statement against pretentiousness and ostentation. Somehow she had unearthed a juggler from France, who wandered around dropping his balls. A flautist tootled sadly on the front porch. Madam Zuleika, who was Alison covered up in a black shawl, read palms as she crouched in a small tent, using a green glass Japanese fishing float as her crystal ball. She promised romance and riches to all comers; isn't that what palm readers are supposed to do?

Doran and Kathy tended a solar oven where a pot of beans cooked very, very slowly. A few borrowed chickens added a homey touch. An anthill sported a sign, "Please leave this alone and do not trample the busy ants in the grass." Did we really hop all round to avoid Doran's damn ants? Could the chickens read? Mary got stung by a wasp and had to take her allergy medicine. The party made $400.

We don't know what Doran's husband said about all this, because Doran and Mike separated soon afterward and Doran headed up-island to tend sheep.

We didn't do much better at later yard sales, because we are not too good at bargaining and sell most of the stuff to each other. Betty's attempt to join the night market scene was probably our nadir. Victoria decided to try an Asian-style market in downtown Centennial Square, a haven for fans of B.C. bud — a famous local strain of marijuana. At last Betty could dispose of a trunkful of Indian fabric, yards and yards of it that reeked of mothballs and competed with the smoke of marijuana. Few customers came, maybe because of the mothballs or because she didn't have the requisite holes pierced in her anatomy to blend in with the crowd. Anyway, she quit, after making $4 and before somebody could come and demand her $10 space rental.

Fundraising wasn't a Granny focus in any case; we were getting distracted.

CSIS, CSIS

Pronounced "see-sis." Sung to the tune of
"Ja-Da," by Bob Carleton, 1918; lyrics by Jane Mackey

CSIS, CSIS, Canadian security.
CSIS, CSIS, watching over you and me.
If you're a union worker who is lonely and blue,
There'll always be somebody who will listen to you.
It's CSIS, CSIS, Canadian security.

CSIS, CSIS, what a bunch of real fun guys.
CSIS, CSIS, protecting us from Commie spies.
Giving up their weekends and working nights,
In spite of being hassled by the Charter of Rights.
Oh, CSIS, CSIS, Canadian security.

CSIS, CSIS, they're a bunch of active snoops.
CSIS, CSIS, infiltrating peaceful groups.
Even 'Raging Grannies 'gainst nuclear subs
Can end up on their list of subversuvs.
Oh, CSIS, CSIS, Canadian security.

TEA AND NO SYMPATHY

*A little more matriarchy is what
the world needs, and I know it.*
— *Dorothy Thompson*

We certainly needed some guidance as we began to venture into other issues of protest and sometimes appeared to lose our way. We strayed into environmental protest. It's no accident that both the Raging Grannies and Greenpeace were spawned on Canada's left coast. It was Greenpeace that encouraged us to join the newly minted Gabriola and Salt Spring Island Grannies in a walk from the Crofton ferry landing to the belching pulp mill operated by the Fletcher Challenge lumber company, in May 1989.

We were attached to blue balloons, which were supposed to represent the eggs of the endangered great blue heron. Apparently, scientists had proved that dioxins, such as those spewing from the plant, were preventing heron eggs from hatching because the shells became too tough? Too soft? Anyway, the herons didn't like it and nor did we. We advanced on the mill, covering our noses with lace hankies against the acrid smell. It was a weekend and the mill manager lived far from the stench so we had to make do with his assistant. We tried to convince him of the rightness of our cause and left him with our clutch of balloon eggs. He didn't seem very appreciative. As we left, an ambulance roared past carrying, we were told, yet another worker overcome by chlorine gas. We never did learn the fate of local herons or what happened to the stricken employee, or our balloons.

We turned our attention to trees. Granny Jean McLaren, from Gabriola, had already been arrested in 1988 trying to stop Fletcher Challenge from dynamiting a road in order to clear-cut a pristine valley. We visited another threatened river valley on Vancouver Island, the Walbran, along with the Western Canada Wilderness Committee, even though it involved a five-hour bus ride and some very slippery mudslides before we actually got to join hands around the endangered giant trees in proper tree-hugger style.

On another occasion, with the Friends of Clayoquot Sound in Tofino, we clambered aboard some very small boats and sailed up an inlet to witness a ceremonial land claim by the local Ahousaht First Nations, far up some mountainside. We were so hot and tired that we fell into the ocean, fully dressed, on our return to the inlet. But we did get our reward — a boat ride to Hot Springs Cove. We stripped and dunked and tried not to giggle at our guide for keeping his hat on, if nothing else.

We'd rather dress up than down, especially for the cameras. Usually we had to be outlandish to get any media, but sometimes we were actually invited to appear on TV. Once they even paid our plane fare to Toronto and our hotel bill, too, at the Royal York, no less. In October 1988, Betty and Linda were picked to represent us on the afternoon TV show, *Lifetime*. We shared billing with Nova Scotian singer Rita MacNeil and a doctor who used bloodsucking leeches in some kind of treatment. We did get a chance to talk briefly about our reasons for protesting as well as to explain our hats and why we had joined the Grannies. Betty owned up to her great-great-grandfather who had marched in the 1837 Rebellion, so we felt we had established some history as well as spread the Granny word.

We had another chance at national TV stardom in November 1989. Mary, Joyce, Fran and Betty got the nod to go to Vancouver to appear on CBC-TV's *Front Page Challenge*. The headline, which moderator Fred Davis called a national story with an element of human interest but a serious side to it, stumped the panel. Probably it was listening to four voices instead of one, and our insistence that we were not entertainers, that perplexed Pierre Berton, Allan Fotheringham, Jack Webster and Betty Kennedy.

After we sang our anti-war-toys song, Berton complained that he didn't consider himself a warmonger just because he had played with lead soldiers and owned a Daisy air rifle in his Yukon boyhood. Fran brought up GI Joe and the fact that kids were learning to use violence to get what they want. Betty Kennedy asked about our marvellous clothes. A Granny suggested that Allan Fotheringham himself would be a good candidate for the Grannies because of his snarky columns in *Maclean's* magazine.

"But that would require a sex change," countered Allan.

"Not at all," Fran shot back. "You could be a Granny-in-drag."

Fred Davis, trying to keep decorum on a family-oriented show, suggested we might sing the last verse of our war-toys song; he graciously ended the program saying that Raging Grannies "obviously care about humanity." We think it was just after this that the *Times Colonist* confirmed we were "a bit of a bomb as pure entertainment."[1] Fotheringham later referred to us as "an amateurish blue-rinse group that plays at charities."[2]

Mike Harcourt, later to become B.C. premier, was another guest on that show. Before the taping, Betty told Harcourt she had walked the streets for Esquimalt NDP candidate Moe Sihota during the previous provincial election. Harcourt said she had better stay out of his Vancouver riding; he had enough streetwalkers there already, thank you very much.

The late Peter Gzowski loved us. We ambushed him at a book-signing at a Victoria mall and his minions signed us up later for a four-way conversation on four separate telephones, into which we sang a very odd rendering of "Here in the Land of the Beaver," totally out of sync. Gzowski had us on his show twice more and seemed fascinated with our clothes. The first time he talked to Bess, it was barely dawn in Victoria and she was happy to describe what she was wearing — not her regular Grannying gear, but her nightie. Next time, when Fran and Bess got promoted to the use of the CBC's tiny studio in the B.C. Legislative Buildings for an interview with Peter, Bess assured him she was not in her nightie this time. Being too much of a gentleman, Peter made no further inquiry.

While we were complaining about war toys, the world was drifting toward a real war. On August 1, 1990, Iraqi troops invaded neighbouring Kuwait. Soon afterward, the United Nations imposed sanctions against Iraq and the next day Saudi Arabia requested help from the United States in countering a possible Iraqi invasion. The U.S. responded with fighter planes and a naval blockade. Operation Desert Shield began to develop into the invasion of Iraq, known as Desert Storm. One by one, United Nations member countries began to consider sending troops. Eventually the U.S. would have 540,000 soldiers, six aircraft carriers, an undisclosed number of submarines, 4,000 tanks, 1,700 helicopters and 1,800 airplanes in what became known as a Rich Man's War and a Poor Man's Fight. Iraq refused to pull back and war began.

In Canada, public acceptance of our country's role in the war was mixed. There were anti-war demonstrations across the country, bringing out 35,000 people. In keeping with the Grannies' agenda of mocking institutions, we went to the Canadian military recruiting office in Victoria at the first hint of mobilization, and presented ourselves front and centre to join up.

"While some may interpret their enlistment attempts as a joke, the Grannies have a serious point to make ... to get the message across that it's unnecessary to risk our boys' lives for oil," said Granny Mary. "They claim it's not for oil, but it is." Mary said many of her classmates had served in World War II and they never came back: "We haven't learned anything in 45 years."[3]

Surprisingly, we all got interviewed by the recruiters and two of us received a call for a second interview. Betty, with a respectable university degree, was one of them. Of course, the recruiting staff were not allowed to ask anybody's age and we weren't going to tell them. In her interview, Betty claimed that she was experienced in conflict resolution, having brought up two children and been married for over 40 years. Jean McLaren sensibly voiced her opinion that "they need some wisdom in the Middle East. Maybe if the Grannies went over there they would talk to us. We don't need to fight over things. It would be a tragedy for Canada's youth to be sacrificed for the oil companies."

Betty kept her appointment with the recruiting officers and found them so agreeable that she withdrew her application and handed them a note, saying, "Sorry for all this stuff by the Grannies but we really don't want to see Canada at war or any young men and women getting killed over the need for oil in the United States."

Instead of Grannies, Canada sent two destroyers, 12 C-130 planes, 24 CF-18 bombers, 4,500 troops and a field hospital. The Royal Canadian Air Force squadron defended coalition ships and participated in bombing runs. There were no Canadian casualties in the 11-week war, but there has been continuing concern over the effects of exposure to depleted uranium, with many veterans suffering from the so-called Gulf War Syndrome. It is estimated that 200,000 Iraqi lives were lost; 35,000 were civilians killed in the bombing of Baghdad alone. Ten thousand Iraqi soldiers were killed when coalition planes bombed their retreat from Kuwait City.

After our attempt that November to discredit Canada's possible participation in a foreign war, there were several indignant letters to the editor. One said, "The Raging Grannies — what hypocrites." The writer resurrected Neville Chamberlain and reminded readers of Chamberlain's promise of "peace in our time" on the eve of World War II. He accused Raging Grannies of posturing. Another suggested, "Grannies: Ship 'em out." This guy asked if he was alone in being underwhelmed by our latest cutesy episode. "Let the

Betty and her teddy bear try to enlist to fight in the first Gulf War. In her interview, she claimed to have experience in conflict resolution, having raised two children and been married for 40 years.

Department of National Defence lower its standards temporarily, recruit the old girls and ship them out to the Persian Gulf."[4]

Canada's leading environmentalist, David Suzuki, was also getting into trouble for registering his concern about the war. Grannies had met Suzuki at the Tin Wis First Nations Conference in Tofino in 1988, and some sponsors were threatening to drop his CBC-TV show *The Nature of Things*, so we rushed to his support.

Jane wrote a "love song" to Suzuki, and even though she had long left the Granny group, she dragged us out to sing it to David while he was at a book-signing in one of the malls.

We love you David, oh yes we do
The world's in trouble, Lord knows it's true
When we feel overwhelmed and blue
We're happy to hear from you.

You're on the radio and TV too
Some people think there's much too much of you
We strongly disagree, indeed we do
'Cause David, we love you.

Keep putting forward your point of view
Voices of sanity are far too few
We're grateful for the work you do
Oh David, we love you.

Suzuki was so busy signing books, it looked as if he wondered, "Who are those women and what on earth are they going on about?" He was, however, all smiles when he comprehended that we were Raging Grannies.

We heard from him later, via handwritten letter, after we had sent him a letter of encouragement: "Ever since the Raging Grannies turned up to serenade me at a book-signing in Victoria, I've been in love with you all. I often cite you as one of the really important groups to make a difference … I am honoured to be supported by you."

We thought we might try a more biblical approach against the Iraq war, especially as Christmas was nearly upon us. With other peace activists we performed a "no room at the inn" nativity play. As wise women, we followed a motley crew of shepherds behind an eight-months-pregnant Mary in procession to the Canadian Forces Base in Esquimalt where, predictably, there was indeed no room at the inn for Mary or for protesters.

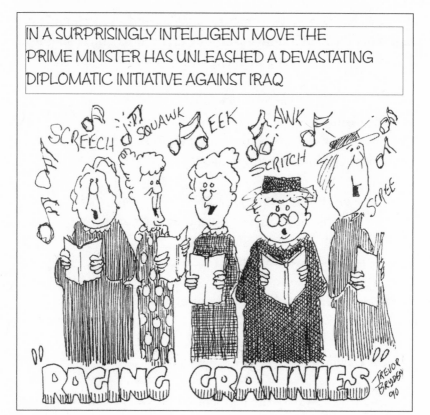

IN A SURPRISINGLY INTELLIGENT MOVE THE PRIME MINISTER HAS UNLEASHED A DEVASTATING DIPLOMATIC INITIATIVE AGAINST IRAQ

RAGING GRANNIES

COURTESY OF TREVOR BRYDEN

Then, at a Granny meeting in December, it was suggested that Grannies join forces with an ad hoc group using body bags in a demonstration just days before local troops left for the Gulf. Consensus at the meeting blocked such an action, but several members of the Raging Grannies took part in it nevertheless. CHEK-TV filmed the whole thing. Victoria was not amused. Neither were some of the Grannies, especially Betty.

"This is Godspeed, not a funeral," thundered a reader in the *Times Colonist*. "Members of one of these peace groups have dressed in homemade body bags for a demonstration outside the Canadian Forces Base, Esquimalt. And a coalition of peace organizations wants waterfront spectators to wear black arm bands when HMCS

Huron sails past today. The peace groups should have directed their pitch to Ottawa in less offensive ways. By tactics such as these they simply alienate public support for their cause.

"Never have I seen anything so sick as was shown on our local TV news on New Year's Eve — so-called pacifists rolling down a hill in Esquimalt in plastic garbage bags. They should have rolled them right off the end of the jetty. Saddam Hussein would love our kooks for the job they are doing."[5]

Then there was the matter of Christmas cards. The public-relations officer at CFB Esquimalt released to the *Esquimalt News* the contents of some Christmas cards that had been passed to departing members of HMCS *Huron* by some protesters.

"You'll be doing the killing, not [Prime Minister Brian] Mulroney. You don't have to go so far to kill and be killed. How will your wife feel if you come back wounded or in a body bag?" wrote one so-called well-wisher. Betty was phoned for a response. "It was an ad hoc group," she said. "Raging Grannies might have been present but unless they were wearing fancy hats they were not representing the rest of us." Acknowledging that the Christmas cards were insensitive, she added, "I think it is wrong of us to attack the base. We must attack the politicians who are making the decisions."[6]

Another letter to the *Times Colonist* commented, "Those of us who are committed to global peace (and that probably means everybody) are inclined to forget the unpleasant truths and must continually remind ourselves that war is NOT flag-waving and send-offs but waste, privation, terror, dismemberment and awful death. The departure of Canadian warships should in truth be marked not only by body bags and black arm bands but also by weeping, lamentation, the rending of clothing and the deepest possible display of grief."[7]

As pre-arranged, several Grannies flew off to an anti-nuclear demonstration at the U.S. nuclear-testing grounds in Nevada. Among the protesters were a number of church members prepared for civil disobedience by entering off-limit areas; their banner read,

"The Church Goes Over the Wire." The local First Nations had their own banner, emblazoned with a silhouette of Elvis Presley, black on red. Elvis was evidently a local icon since he was himself part native and quite a mover and shaker. The protesters pulled down a section of the fence around the test site and disappeared into the desert, to be rounded up an hour later by a private security company and dumped in the nearest town, without being charged. We were too chicken to go along with them, not wanting to get lost in the desert or to be arrested as Canadians in a foreign country. We also confess that we played the slot machines when we got back to Las Vegas, but we can't all be perfect, can we? Upon hearing the latest news of impending war with Iraq, Alison proposed that our Granny gaggle could be a contact should any young Americans need an underground railway system to escape a draft call. "They could say they were coming to visit their grandmas," she suggested.

By the time the Grannies returned from Nevada, war fever was raging throughout the western world and the peace movement was reacting everywhere. Petitions were signed. Grannies returned to the recruitment centre for a "knit-in," occupying the reception centre and taking up all the chairs with furious but inexpert knitters. Demonstrators pounded on empty oil drums on the streets of downtown Victoria. The symbols and the images, the sound and the fury, were exceedingly warlike.

"Drummer Beats Empty Oil Drums as 250 Victorians Condemn War. After a well-attended forum in a downtown church called by a Mideast coalition of peace groups, demonstrators, including Raging Grannies, emerged to block traffic in downtown Victoria."[8] We were proud that Granny Hilda Marczak was one of the organizers of the coalition that brought church and peace groups together.

Two days later, demonstrations were held at the University of Victoria, Camosun College and several high schools. Students downed books and converged at the corner of Yates and Douglas streets. A roaring cheer went up as the groups combined and milled around briefly amid startled shoppers. Then the assemblage swept

The Grannies protested at a nuclear-weapons test site in Nevada, then, after our work was done, we went to Las Vegas to play the slots.

down Douglas Street toward the B.C. legislature. Pounding drums followed, one of them banged by Doran and Kathy. Police held back the traffic at each intersection. Students climbed up and hung white flags from the bayonet brandished by the bronze Canadian soldier on the Cenotaph on the lawn of the legislature. It had been a near-riot, but police reaction had been exemplary and eventually the crowd dispersed.

That same evening, thousands joined a candlelight vigil at the Cenotaph. In the cold and darkness we chanted over and over again John Lennon and Paul McCartney's song "Give Peace a Chance."

Several hundred students tramped off to the military base in Esquimalt to sit silently in front of the closed gates. The next day,

Grannies joined a group from Conscience Canada to go to the Revenue Canada office and demand to know how much of our income tax was going to pay for war. We were met by officers from the Canadian Security and Intelligence Service (CSIS). There were no answers from the tax people, although we did get inside their office. We were televised but the film was never shown. The war began that night.

When Iraq fired the first Scud missiles into Israel, public attitudes to our protests began to change: if our country was at war, any protest could be seen as subversive. We might be appalled at the greedy arms industry, at a war that targeted civilians, at crippling the infrastructure of a country, at destroying hundreds of oil wells and polluting the Persian Gulf, but it was not wise to say so.

After the Americans attacked Iraq, the University Women's Club of Victoria cancelled its invitation to us to sing at one of its meetings. Protests against the war were indeed low-key. Betty was convinced that the starch had been taken out of the Grannies and out of the peace movement. Alison thought it had just gone underground. Betty and her husband went off on a Caribbean cruise, her barbed comments against the war with Iraq and the destruction of Baghdad embarrassing her husband and making her very unpopular with the American travellers who shared their dinner table. Soon the fighting stopped but sanctions against Iraq followed. As we were to find in the years to come, that war never really ended.

We quickly had evidence that protests were becoming unwelcome. The Raging Grannies had actually been invited in November to entertain the crowds expected downtown in Victoria on New Year's Eve at an alcohol-free First Night. Then the invitation was withdrawn when someone in the First Night organization decided we were not just entertainers. They offered us a "non-performance" fee of $200 — much more than we had ever been offered for singing. Producer Mary Sparacio said, "The onus of making equal time available to other groups with a political message is a responsibility I take seriously" — which we think was a real cop-out.

"Hush money offer strikes sour chord with Grannies," said the *Times Colonist* headline. "Victoria's First Night organization wants to pay the Raging Grannies to clam up ... fearing they would be too 'political.'"[9] The First Night producer, with a bizarre reversal of logic, referred to the Grannies as "the fascist song police."[10] Alison responded that "even Good King Wenceslas had a social message." A letter to the editor of *Monday Magazine,* Victoria's alternative weekly, from a First Night performer said that "the exclusion of the Grannies was itself an affront to such community standards as peace, a cleaner environment and the activism that defends them."[11]

The Grannies went out to First Night celebrations anyway and sang to the lineups outside the legitimate performances. Maybe that's where we fit in best. And the $200 "non-performance fee"? We can't remember whether we refused it or accepted it and passed it on to one of our favourite non-profit groups working for the needy folk downtown.

So much for entertaining. Instead, we decided to target those irksome nuclear vessels again. In 1992 we even got Victoria's Mayor David Turner and MP John Brewin to go to Ogden Point with us to protest another arrival, but we got no response from the ship's captain. Then we heard that the USS *Texas*, a huge, nuclear-powered, guided-missile cruiser, was about to arrive at CFB Esquimalt. They even announced an open house. What an opportunity.

The *Neptune Papers*, research documents produced by Greenpeace, told us all we needed to know about the *Texas*: "Eight Tomahawks are carried in two four-celled armoured box launchers. Two nuclear reactors power each [vessel]."[12] We Grannies do our research.

Open house! Wow, we thought, what a place for a tea party. We stuffed a teapot, milk, sugar, cups and saucers into our purses. Alison embroidered a pale green tablecloth with the slogan "Tea Not Tomahawks." We alerted the press and off we went. Of course, our flamboyant hats and noisy chatter identified us easily to the

CFB guard at the gate, but he waved our cars through and only asked, "Are you going to sing?"

We parked and walked down the slope to the warship. Betty noticed us getting interested looks from plainclothes guys with guns on their hips and walkie-talkies in their hands. Even so, we were greeted in the customary fashion with a blast from a bosun's whistle as we came aboard. We were almost persuaded to take the guided tour, since there was no sign of any media arriving. By heavens, the ship was big. Betty had failed to say in her news release where, on the ship, our tea party would take place. The announced time of 2 P.M. was almost upon us, and no press!

"To heck with the media," said Fran, who had been designated to give the go-ahead signal. "We have to do this thing regardless." We asked a nearby sailor to take a handwritten invitation to the captain to join us for tea. The sailor would tell him where. We had decided to use the "blunt" end of the ship for our tea party — more deck space and no Tomahawk launcher being demonstrated there. A couple of us, desperate to find the press, spotted a *Times Colonist* photographer scurrying along behind a storming captain and his horrified staff. Old ladies having tea on his battleship? Unthinkable. The photographer discreetly signalled the Grannies to get a move on. By the time the captain and his officers, all in dress uniforms with a lot of gold braid, arrived, Alison had the tablecloth spread out on the deck and Fran was pouring tea, or pretending to. (Even Grannies cannot transport liquid tea in our purses, though the cookies were real.) Nancy Brown, the reporter, looked totally professional, scribbling notes, as if this sort of thing happened all the time. Alex Barta, the photographer, climbed over ropes and stanchions to get the light behind him. (No photograph in the paper next day. Maybe there wasn't enough light after all.) Nobody, but nobody, was laughing. This tea party was a dead serious breach of protocol.

The captain snatched up our beautiful tablecloth.

"That is a political slogan," he barked.

"That is a tablecloth," Alison claimed.

"I want you to leave my ship," he ordered Alison, but meaning the whole lot of misguided women.

"But why? We only want to take afternoon tea with you."

"Not Tomahawks," Fran piped up.

By now the Canadian base commander had arrived, also resplendent in navy blue and gold. Accompanying him were two of his staff officers. The American captain asked him to "please remove these women from my ship. At once." The etiquette between the two NATO members in a time of international crisis was admirable.

Betty's husband later asked her if we had been marched off by sailors carrying their guns "at half slope," meaning we were under arrest. But not at all. We had a very friendly, chatty sort of stroll to the gangplank, which we walked down sedately, quite relieved not to be dumped in the harbour. We did receive a good-for-you grin and a thumbs-up signal of approval from an American sailor as we passed him, but a woman who worked at the base thumbed her nose at us as we disembarked.

Once we were on Canadian soil, the dock itself, we were chastised by the base commander, who accused us of abusing U.S. and Canadian government hospitality. Fran, ever the counsellor, countered that she heard anger in his voice. He denied it and the discussion that followed was peppered with a lot of "Excuse me's" and "If you will just allow me to finish ..." Of course, neither side yielded an inch. There was little common ground and a lot of rhetoric and sophistry flying.

"They are abusing Canadian hospitality by bringing weapons of mass destruction into Canada," Mary insisted. The American captain had told us on the ship that it is up to Canada's Department of National Defence to respond to a nuclear accident. "He's only concerned about his ship, not about us," she said.

The issue of Canadian sovereignty came up and seventh-generation Canadians Mary and Betty were horrified that the Canadian navy seemed complicit in U.S. defence strategy that saw Canada as part of Fortress America. With NATO, NORAD and

NAFTA, Canada seemed already on the way to becoming the 51st state.

We did agree with the base commander that our Canada is a great place to live and if Grannies carried on in some parts of the world as we do here, they'd have been popped into jail long before now. But that was beside the point. We carried on walking to our cars accompanied by a naval lieutenant, a sergeant in the military police and a military police car bringing up the rear. We were rewarded in the *Times Colonist* the next day: "*Texas* is no place for tea, Grannies escorted off ship."[13] There was no photo of us, but instead a scary photo of the surface-to-air Tomahawk-missile-launching system on the warship, obvious proof that we Grannies knew whereof we protested.

By 1992, we were getting a bit tired from all this activity, and the media were getting a bit tired of us. Adrian Chamberlain, the *Times Colonist*'s entertainment writer, put down his New Year's wish as "never having to hear the Raging Grannies sing again."[14] We were heading for trouble.

TAKE ME OUT TO THE CLEAR-CUT

Sung to the tune of "Take Me Out to the Ball Game,"
by Jack Norworth and Albert Tilzer, 1908; lyrics by Hub Meeker

Take me out to the clear-cut. We'll picnic on a few stumps.
I want you to know I'm a tree-farming nut
Who thinks like a chainsaw that's stuck in a rut.
MacBloedel * gets a hip-hooray. They make black picnic
    grounds pay.
So it's one makes it two. Dear Investors, thank you,
You have spruced up our day.

Take me out to the clear-cut. The timber's been tidied away.
It's been sold down the stream in a businessman's dream.
It's swell to stand here on a landscape so clean.
So it's off to lumbering elsewhere. I'll lumber you and you me.
It's the buzz of the mill that produces the thrill
Worth a thousand trees.

* Change the name of the timber company to suit.

ON THE ROAD, THROUGH THE WOODS AND INTO TROUBLE

If you obey all the rules, you miss all the fun.
— *Katherine Hepburn*

Maybe some other folks would find us new and different. And maybe we'd get along together better on the road. In August 1991, when we were invited to both the Kaslo Summer School of the Arts and to a women's workshop in Nelson, and the school was even offering us an honorarium of $270, off we went — Alison, Anne, Betty and Joyce packed into Alison's Toyota Tercel, along with sleeping bags, bathing suits and towels, food, Anne's special sleeping pillow, four large Granny hats, costumes and lots of ideas. This was our first songwriting workshop but there would be many more.

We tell our students that our songs — and we have more than 150 of them — usually start from a need. When we must have a song protesting such causes as the renewal of the grizzly bear hunt in British Columbia, or Victoria's latest edict against panhandling, Alison, or one of our other budding lyricists, produces a draft and everybody says what's wrong with it. Sometimes we junk it altogether. Mostly, the chorus of suggested changes produces a much better song in the end, so the songwriter learns to grow a thick skin.

The melodies we use range from folk tunes to the Beatles' compositions. We dredge up hymns from childhood and early pop songs from a romantic adolescence, though our repertoire is hopelessly out of date. And since we are probably the worst singers of all the Granny groups, we don't attempt anything difficult. Some other groups sang together in an opera chorus, for heaven's sake. If desperate, we may resort to learning the melody from a tape but we're really safest with "Daisy, Daisy." It helps when one of us conducts, but we never seem to practise hard enough or take enough care with our diction, though Anita, our eldest Granny, keeps urging us to enunciate like Noel Coward.

For us, no song is sacred — especially not hymns, although other groups draw the line at using religious melodies. Sometimes, if the tune eludes us, we'll just speak the words — loudly.

At one time, a determined Granny tried to get us to chirp like ladies and stop braying like fishwives. She kept telling us to pinch our buttock cheeks together to get our voices into the upper ranges, while we insisted on keeping our pitch low so we could shout out the message. We never did master the buttocks bit; that Granny never mastered us, and soon left.

If our singing lacks quality, the lyrics pack a punch and often cause more respectable Grannies to tut-tut. At one Unconvention the Toronto group nearly came to blows over whether or not to sing the song we had written soon after the revelation of Bill Clinton's trysts with Monica Lewinsky, a song in which we confessed that every one of us had slept with William Lyon Mackenzie King (a decidedly deceased prime minister). We try to be cheeky, though some would say we epitomize bad taste.

The songs that work best for us are short and snappy, with words that relate to those of the original song: for instance, "Missiles keep falling on our heads" from that raindrop song in *Butch Cassidy and the Sundance Kid*. Alison, still our chief doer of ditties, pores over her rhyming dictionary, wishing she were W. S. Gilbert or Ogden

Nash. The worst rhyme she can remember using was in a song about Lorena Bobbitt and her hapless mate, where she rhymed "had enough" with "chop it off."

On the way to our inaugural songwriting workshop, we spent the first night in Greenwood, thanks to Shirley and Jim Fyles, long-time peace activists. When we walked beyond their garden to the recently abandoned Kettle Valley Railroad, we collected a quantity of railroad spikes. Jim had turned some of them into wind chimes, so we loaded up the car with our collection of spikes, planning to string them onto bars as wind chimes, as he did, and sell them later as a fundraising effort in Victoria. (We painted them up and Betty and Alison tried their best to sell them but not one sold, maybe because they were so heavy it would take a gale to make them chime. Eventually, Joyce interested the Victoria Historical Society in them and we did make some profit.)

The second day we got as far as Inger's cabin in the woods, in Argenta. Originally a Quaker community, Argenta still has the aura of 1900, with an overlay of the 1960s. Summer roads are mere paths, the trees make tunnels over them and water comes from upstream via gravity, as long as somebody remembers to throw in a few rocks when the pressure gets low. Inger's summer responsibilities were to collect manure from the cows, which were pegged out overnight in the communal pasture, and fertilize the peas, carrots, spinach and raspberries. We went on a walkabout, learning about the bears, the cougars and the mosquitoes. An orchard sloped downhill to evergreen trees and beyond them were the mountains. We met Hugh Elliott, the creator of the community's electrical system, and a number of artists and craftsfolk, and swam in the buff — not a soul around, just blue sky, warm water and soft, soft sand. Joyce and Anne stayed at a nearby bed and breakfast. Alison and Betty bunked down in an empty, two-room house belonging to Betty Tillotson. Alison — always anxious to keep the peace — slept on the floor; Betty got the bed.

The next morning we got to Kaslo, met a dedicated group of local women and prepared for our workshop and performance.

We wanted to earn that $270. The workshop turned out to be less difficult than we had feared, with Joyce and Alison doing the talking and Betty — the one with the best handwriting — chalking everything up on the blackboard. In fact, the women who attended the workshop surprised us with their ability to isolate several local problems and write a song together. Inger organized all the hats, shawls, aprons and wigs we had amassed. A volunteer wrote down the newborn songs and made copies; somebody phoned the local newspaper and yes, a photographer would love to come to our planned protest against local logging.

One elderly woman took a Granny aside, saying she had recently remarried and she wasn't sure her new husband would approve of her making a fool of herself on the main street. Another one decided this sort of thing was not her cup of tea. Grannies stood back to let the newly launched group take to the streets, to a mostly favourable response and a few male boos. The next week's *Kaslo Times* had a photograph and an article that balanced the protesters' concerns with those of the logging company they were protesting. It seemed a noble effort to help prevent a clear-cut in the local mountains, or at least to make folks think twice about the wisdom of such a thing.

We were even invited back two years later, when we branched out into hat-making, palmistry and the interpretation of dreams, with typical Granny lack of expertise. Since then, the women of Argenta have formed their own Granny group and one of the Kaslo women has moved to Santa Rosa, California, where she set up another gaggle. We are indeed infectious.

When the afternoon protest in Kaslo was over, the Grannies again went for a swim, clothed this time. It was a remarkably lovely place with green willows along the shore that shielded our "changing room" as we donned our bathing suits. High mountains densely covered with forest formed a backdrop and a full moon was already visible in the sky at sunset. It didn't seem possible that some greedy profiteer might be intending to destroy all this beauty that had taken so long to create.

After supper at the best local restaurant we returned to the Langham Cultural Centre, where we were to be the entertainment after an academic book launch. The theatre was like an oven; the new book was about some abstruse aspect of an American poet — linking him with Freud or somebody. Mind you, the assembled group all looked pretty academic themselves, and the Grannies wondered how on earth we would be received.

Wine and cheese followed the author's dissertation and in the cooler evening air Grannies thought there would be no audience — returning to that sweatbox of a theatre seemed crazy. But we were wrong. Most people did come back and received the Grannies with unsurpassed generosity. We were a hit! We rather wished then that we had a book to sell, too.

Next morning we were up early to start for the women's conference, but first there was a fabulous breakfast. Bruce Farley made pancakes to accompany Mary Farley's homemade raspberry jam. He had already made plates of hot muffins. Betty slavered at the eastern American antiques in the house — pine cupboards, corner cupboards, a pie cupboard with fancy tin doors, old dolls, lamps, tables, all enhancing a perfectly designed house. There were lots of windows for looking outside at the garden full of flowers and some fancy, fluffy chickens and a friendly dog.

Fortified by breakfast, the group, in two cars this time, drove off for the conference centre outside Nelson. Inger's map didn't work so well here, but after travelling around in several circles we reached our destination, somewhat surprised to be greeted by a number of bare-breasted women in jeans. We learned this was to be a "Wymyn's" conference, with a preponderance of lesbian participants. We tried to be nonchalant, though some of us gulped a little. The women at our songwriting workshops were gracious in accepting advice from visiting crones, and when our students sang their song about a recent gay bashing in the valley, they got wild applause.

Leaving for Nelson for the night, we found that the lights on Inger's Volvo had gone out but we managed somehow to reach our motel. Then we headed for Victoria, but on the way Joyce scared us to death by freezing when trying to pass a logging truck. We had to yell at her to put on the brakes and we didn't let her drive again.

A great road trip. When we did it again in 1993 Alison's tent collapsed with us inside, and Fran and Inger had words because Fran's dog left a calling card in Inger's garden. Fran insisted that she always knew when the dog was about to poop; Inger didn't believe her. Alison and Betty were more concerned about the bear scat liberally sprinkled in the woods close by.

Back home, we took to the water again, but not to chase nuclear vessels. First, we were stupid enough to enter a charity rowing race in Victoria Harbour, and found ourselves in a heavy navy whaler, facing backwards and totally incapable of aiming in the right direction. We came in third; there were only three boats in the race. Then we decided to join the first paddling marathon from Sechelt to Nanaimo, organized by the Georgia Strait Alliance of environmental groups. On the entry form, under "Sex" we checked the box for "Male" and wrote "Yes, please" and added that we intended to go "All the way" in the event. But when we found out that it meant crossing 30 kilometres of open sea in kayaks and canoes, we thought again. We tried using open umbrellas as sails, but again that meant going backwards or being unable to see where we were heading. Finally we gave up and decided to become a welcoming committee instead, paddling out from Piper's Lagoon in Nanaimo to encourage the more stalwart entrants.

We did somewhat better at chasing the USS *Leftwich* at Ogden Point in Victoria Harbour, probably because Greenpeace members were with us and they had a megaphone and a plan — to spray-paint anti-nuclear signs on the battleship's sides. Greenpeace swooped in close. The U.S. sailors turned their hose full-force on the first Zodiac as another roared in. Alison, in her four-metre kayak, *Lucy*, paddled as close as she dared and shouted, "Don't you pee on me, young man. Does your mother know what you do for a living?" The wake slopped into *Lucy*, the water turning pink with the dye from Alison's red feather boa. But Mary paddled up in her kayak to assist, while from the dock

Fran and Betty used the megaphone to belt out Granny songs across the water.

When we returned, soggily, with Greenpeace, we learned that the open house at Ogden Point planned for that afternoon had been cancelled. Maybe they were beginning to get our message but it was becoming harder to get to the right targets.

We tried again. On Mother's Day, 1992, we learned that the USS *Jefferson City*, a nuclear-powered submarine that might be carrying nuclear weapons, had arrived in Esquimalt Harbour. We phoned and faxed the media, loaded our kayaks and canoes with withered flowers for the sailors — a reverse Mother's Day presentation — and paddled forth. Surprise! No submarine. What went wrong?

When the Grannies and Greenpeace (Alison in her kayak, Greenpeace in a Zodiac) protested the USS Leftwich *at Ogden Point, the navy responded with full-force hoses. Alison shouted, "Don't you pee on me, young man. Does your mother know what you do for a living?"*

In the same protest against the USS Leftwich, *Alison and Mary are seen here in kayaks. The ship was a destroyer capable of carrying Tomahawk cruise missiles.*

We decided there were five possibilities:

a) The U.S. Navy heard about us and cancelled. This is known as the delusion-of-grandeur syndrome.

b) The Department of National Defence gave out wrong information, which was unlikely, as they had never lied to us before.

c) Our friend who did the phoning from the Greater Victoria Disarmament Group got the message wrong, which was possible.

d) The submarine was actually in Nanoose Bay, just north of Nanaimo, also possible.

e) It had come and gone before we got launched. We should have checked.

Next day we did check and found that answer e) was correct. Maybe they left early to avoid our singing.

Another time we tried to welcome the sailors of the USS *Abraham Lincoln* with an advertisement in the naval base newspaper, inviting them to meet us at Captain Cook's statue, on Victoria's Inner Harbour, to discuss the hazards of radiation. Our ad was rejected and the Vancouver *Province* took notice: "Thumbs down to CFB Esquimalt's newspaper, *Lookout*, for nuking a small ad the Raging Grannies wanted to put in the base paper for today's Victoria arrival of the nuclear-powered aircraft carrier USS *Abraham Lincoln*. The harmless ad, headed, 'Hi Sailor,' promotes a little get-together the Grannies are organizing tomorrow for *Abraham Lincoln* sailors. 'Sorry, no political ads,' said base spokeswoman Lieutenant Nathalie Garcia. The Grannies just wanted to chat about the dangers of nuclear power and weapons. Surely, the sailors are entitled to hear them."[1]

Hi Sailor

Why not join us for tea and tantalizing talk!
Learn all about it from your Raging Grannies!
About what? You need to ask?
Come along sailor, you'll find out!
Where? Under the Captain Cook statue across
from the Empress Hotel on Government Street.
When? Saturday, March 24 noon
to 2:00 PM

See ya sailor!

This was the ad inviting the sailors of the USS Abraham Lincoln *to discuss the hazards of radiation. The naval base newspaper,* Lookout, *refused to run it, and the Vancouver* Province *took note.*

If the U.S. Navy and our own Department of National Defence weren't listening, why not go to court? In 1992, urged on by Anne, we signed affidavits in support of the Vancouver Island Peace Society's federal court challenge to the legality of nuclear warships entering Canadian ports. We were joined by 38 other citizens, including MPs, MLAs, ex-military officers, physicians, a First Nations chief, the mayor of Victoria and then-leader of the federal New Democratic Party, Audrey McLaughlin. We were in good company.

Betty, using Freedom of Information sources, appended a hefty copy of the Canadian Forces Base Esquimalt Nuclear Emergency Response Plan to her 13-page affidavit, noting that samples from the water surrounding visiting nuclear vessels had to be sent to

The Grannies greet then-leader of the NDP Audrey McLaughlin, visiting Victoria in 1992. (ALEX BARTA/VICTORIA *TIMES COLONIST* PHOTO)

Vancouver for radioactivity tests, and these could take days and days. Besides, Esquimalt still had no adequate emergency plan. Alison drew attention to the possibility of radioactive coolant leaking from nuclear vessels in other areas, and wondered if she was safe paddling her kayak around Esquimalt Harbour.

Some of us trundled up to Nanaimo to present our affidavits in person and to sing our atomic submarine song to the tune, of course, of the Beatles' "Yellow Submarine." It took a year for the federal court to render its judgment, which refused to overturn cabinet orders or force an environmental review. Later, the Supreme Court of Canada refused to hear an appeal, but we believe the effort was worth it because we had alerted a large section of the public to the dangers of visits by nuclear ships.

Those annoying submarines were one issue that all Victoria Grannies could agree on, but we were getting more disagreeable with each other. Sociologists would say that we were floundering in our group relationship. Differences had been apparent from the beginning. In February 1988, Fran wrote a paper about the group for her university course, explaining that "on one hand it looks dysfunctional, while on the other hand it is highly successful in accomplishing one of its tasks: to educate the unconverted through its performances. It hasn't been so successful with its other goal of forming a support group that would help them all during their periods of burn-out." We should have taken that warning seriously.

At all five meetings that Fran studied, there was unresolved conflict among five strong-willed potential leaders and insecurity among the others. Asked what they enjoyed about being Grannies, members mentioned camaraderie, singing, dressing up, networking, friendship, bouncing off ideas, the interplay of personalities and the audience response. But, reported Fran, the list of what they *didn't* like was longer: "Always having to sing, not practising what we preach, personal conflicts, not listening to each other, ill-feeling, talking about others behind their backs, manipulation, everyone talking at once, criticizing each other, power politics, ego building or ego bashing, the decision-making process, poor feedback, defensiveness and apologies, lack of respect, fear of confrontation, lack of understanding of the consensus process." A formidable list.

Indeed, many a Granny meeting broke up in tears, and even more led to shouting. We tried for a time to use a talking stick, which was handed round and would allow only the Granny with the stick in her hand to talk, but even passing the stick around became too dangerous at close quarters. There were complaints that Hilda treated us like kindergarten kids, that we didn't do enough practising or that we did too much, that Joyce sulked, that Alison was impatient, that Doran's ideas were too weird. Betty was lucky; she could turn down her hearing aids when the noise got too bad. All those determined women could be very stubborn. Everybody enjoyed the actions; it was the discussions that began to get us down. Yes, we did laugh a lot, even at ourselves, but there were hurt feelings underneath much of the laughter.

In 1993, open conflict broke out. Its immediate cause was the proposed writing of a book about the Grannies. Some Grannies wanted it to be a sort of *Whole Earth Catalogue*, with offerings about anything from every Granny, without benefit of editing. Alison, who had had two books published, and Betty, with lots of articles to her credit, didn't believe any good book would result from such a free-for-all. They struggled with a manuscript that included autobiographies and ideas from the other Grannies, but a group of Grannies vetoed it and went to see the prospective publisher. That was the end of the book and almost the end of the Victoria Grannies.

We brought in a lawyer as a mediator and spent most of a day rehashing mutual complaints without any agreement. Doran, Kathy, Joyce, Hilda, Lois and Linda quit. We still chat with them when we see them at demonstrations, and we have long gotten over our spat, putting it down to different agendas and personality conflicts, but we probably all share the blame for being pigheaded. At the time of the split some of us were devastated because if we couldn't keep a spirit of peaceful co-operation within our group, who were we to preach peace to others? Only five Grannies were left: Alison, Betty, Fran, Inger and Mary. Would we survive?

Just when we were feeling so depleted, we got two new, strong members and we were handed a major cause, this time a monumental attack on the environment. Three of us would be arrested and two would go to jail for trying to save the trees during Canada's largest act of civil disobedience — the Clayoquot War in the Woods, 1993.

Ria Bos was a landscape gardener, so no wonder she was our chief environmentalist. She had encountered the Grannies in downtown Victoria a year before but was told the group was full and she'd have to wait. In 1993, we needed her.

Ria grew up in Holland and still remembers the Canadian soldier who gave her a chocolate bar as the Allied troops pressed the Nazis back in World War II. She married a Dutchman and they immigrated to Canada. He believed that the wife's place was in their new home, which is where she stayed, frustrated and discontent. When her husband found another partner and her four children reached adulthood and moved out, Ria decided her chance to speak up for herself and for her beliefs had come.

We always loved going to Ria's for meetings because she is a great cook and fabric artist. She fed us strawberries and green peas from her bountiful garden and she always had some new and wonderful tapestry or sculpture to show us. She made our best banner, the one with a scarlet Raging Granny raising her fist against injustice, war or whatever. Ria worked for years as a landscaper, but found that nobody wanted her just to design a garden; they wanted her to dig, and arthritis was making digging a very painful affair. Being a Raging Granny took just as much energy but was easier on the knees.

Ria says her most important gig was when her 16-year-old grandson, Michael, invited her to school in Edmonton for "show and tell." Michael's mother bought her a plane ticket and on the appointed day Ria and Michael were dropped off at his school. She asked if he would prefer that she not wear her hat, wondering if he really wanted to go through with the idea and saying she would never have been brave enough to invite her own grandmother to school. But he was cool about the hat and his classmates were enthusiastic about her presentation, even if it went overtime.

Reaching young people was what Ria enjoyed most about Grannying. She did not like the meetings; in fact, for the last few years she hasn't attended a single one. She is now one of our auxiliary Grannies, singing with us sometimes at rallies. Do we ever miss going to her house — especially the fresh strawberries.

Anita Bundy, our oldest Granny, came next. She sat next to Mary Rose at a disarmament potluck supper and auction, asked how she could join the Grannies and was slipped a paper napkin to write her name and phone number. Two weeks went by and she had almost given up when Mary called to invite her to a meeting, which was in Ria's living room. She recalls debating what to wear, but she needn't have worried, because she found a flock of Grannies in sweat pants or jeans, though Betty wore a dress and pearls.

"The room was in chaos, everybody talking at once," Anita recalls, "interrupting, contradicting, shouting." She meekly suggested we use a talking stick or even Robert's Rules of Order and was immediately shouted down. Ten years later, she reports, nothing has changed. "I love it," says Anita.

Anita started out as a good convent girl born to conservative parents in Winnipeg. They even voted Conservative. She went to Anglican Church Sunday school, got confirmed, and passed round goodies at church teas. But when she went to the University of Manitoba and found liberal, even radical, thinkers, Anita was baptized into rebellion, though it was still all talk, she says. What she remembers more than the rhetoric was dancing and romancing — formal balls, corsages with Shakespearean sonnets attached, midnight suppers, goodnight kisses and longing for more. She had a fairy-tale wedding to a man who "looked like an Adonis." He went off to World War II and was never the same; he died in 1986.

Anita worked for 30 years at the Anglican Church headquarters in Toronto, and it was there she learned how to protest, when to protest and whom to protest to. She raged against multinational corporations, apartheid, pollution, the banks and the government. So when she moved to Victoria in 1991, she was ideal Granny material. We don't mind that we are not allowed to hold meetings in her oceanside apartment because her neighbours are picky about noise; she often makes up for her inhospitality by taking us all out for lunch.

She doesn't cook, so a Granny who went on a mission of mercy when Anita was ailing had to take an entire library out of the oven before she could heat up a meal for the patient. We forgive her for hoarding old paper serviettes to use for cleaning the floor, for stocking her refrigerator with doggy bags from restaurants, for hanging a "Do Not Resuscitate" label round her neck in case she passes out but doesn't "croak," as she so elegantly puts it. In her mid-80s, she is our most elegant Granny, still with jet-black hair that she adorns with a sparkly hair band. She's a fanatical fan of the CBC and a ferocious foe of certain members of the Canadian government. She is the only one of us who has held out against computer technology and regales us each week with her epic struggles to tame her VCR.

Ria and Anita were very useful additions; we needed numbers in our fight to save the trees. Long before 1993 we had protested clear-cut logging. Our song, "Take Me Out to the Clear-Cut," written by Fran's partner, Hub Meeker, in 1990, is still one of our favourites. And the War in the Woods had started long before that.

First, a little history. Clayoquot Sound, on the wet — and wild — side of Vancouver Island, is home to the largest lowland temperate rainforest left in a world that has already destroyed most of the forests that are its lungs. In Clayoquot, the tallest trees tower as high as a 30-storey skyscraper; they were there before Christopher Columbus sailed west. And they're "ours." They grow on Crown land, though it is leased to forest companies through tree farm licences — in those days to MacMillan Bloedel and Interfor.

The Friends of Clayoquot Sound came together in 1979 when MacBlo revealed its plans to clear-cut half of Meares Island. The

Friends were ready, with the First Nations and the press, when the loggers arrived. They did save Meares Island but had to turn out again in 1988 to stop Fletcher Challenge, a global forestry company based in New Zealand, from dynamiting a road through Sulphur Pass to the pristine Megan valley, northeast of Tofino. Jean McLaren, a Gabriola Island Granny, was one of the protesters arrested. We sent letters of objection and then breathed a sigh of relief when an NDP government took over in 1991.

Imagine our surprise then, when, in April 1993, the NDP approved MacBlo's plan to cut down 74 percent of the old-growth trees in Clayoquot Sound. We didn't want to believe it, so we drove up to Tofino to check things out with the Friends of Clayoquot Sound. Their tiny office had just been vandalized. The War in the Woods had begun, but we didn't really want to climb trees or chain ourselves to logging trucks. We wouldn't give up on the democratic process, not yet.

So, like good little citizens, we asked for a meeting with Minister of Forests Dan Miller. We gave him a time and date, called the press and took along our knitting in case we had to wait. Miller took one look at the cameras and invited us in, but no coffee and no concessions. He was not a man to change his mind, he said.

Next we invited the CEO of MacBlo to come to a tea party. Nobody could say we had closed minds. We even offered to pay his helicopter fare, crossing our fingers that we wouldn't actually have to cough up. Instead he sent us Linda Coady, his director of government relations. She arrived wearing a power suit, high-heeled pumps and a very practised smile. We had "borrowed" Sharon Chow from the Sierra Club who knew a lot more about environmental problems in the logging industry than any of us. She also had recent photos of MacBlo's clear-cuts to show to Linda. All we could do was agree to disagree, but Linda did whisper to one of us on her departure, "Be careful or you'll be in real trouble. This is going to get serious." Eight days later we were standing at the Kennedy Lake Road bridge, waiting for the logging trucks and the Royal Canadian Mounted Police.

We like to think we did have some influence on Linda, because she was later named vice-president of environmental enterprise for MacBlo's purchasers, Weyerhaeuser, and played a major role in agreements to bring peace to the woods. Now she works for World Wildlife Fund Canada.

While we were talking politely to Linda, protesters had begun swarming to the peace camp set up by the Friends of Clayoquot Sound in a blackened clear-cut close to the Kennedy Lake Road. They came from Europe, from the U.S., from Australia. The camp cook, Guido Kettler, arrived on holiday from Switzerland, intending to stay for a day, and stayed all summer. A train full of protesters from Ottawa, bound for Clayoquot, arrived in Vancouver and made their way to Vancouver Island. Among those who visited the camp were artists and loggers, a priest, an MP, professors and librarians and hundreds of young people — and their dogs. The youngest to face arrest was Adam Harris, aged 10; the oldest was Summer Pemberton, aged 81. So many people wanted to join the protest that the Friends organized special days for women, for young people and, finally, for seniors. That would be us: August 19. Three older women, Inessa Ormond, Judith Robinson and Betty Krawczyk, had already been arrested and were languishing in jail because they would not sign an agreement to stay away from the protest. How could *we* stay away?

It was a group decision for everyone to go and support Ria and Alison, the ones willing to be arrested, because a supporter to pick them up when they were released from the detention centre was just as important as those being arrested. Inger was at her cabin in Argenta and would have to wait until September to make her stand.

Being Grannies, we were going to do it in style. Jean McLaren was spending the whole summer in camp, teaching peaceful civil disobedience and sleeping on a rock. We didn't do rocks. Instead, we booked into a nearby cheap motel, came down to the camp to get our training and lingered around the fire, listening to the concerns about chores and noise and learning the technique of "twinkling" with the fingers to signify agreement instead of applauding, so as not to disturb the speaker.

Everyone seemed so young. The security team, armed with a smile against vandals, couldn't have been more than 17. Toddlers and dogs wandered through the camp, everyone was grubby, nobody seemed to be giving orders and yet everything was under control, even dinner. We had brought up veggies from Ria's garden and cake donated by one of the many Victoria businesses supporting the blockade, but surely this was the miracle of loaves and fishes, as more than a hundred people loaded up their plates and there was even coffee. Later we learned that more than 10,000 people visited the camp that summer and went home with a useful education. We drove back to the motel and set our alarm clocks for 4 A.M.

Sure enough it was cold, dark and raining when we drove back to camp. Flashlights flickered, car lights came on and we joined a silent procession driving up the logging road toward the bridge. Some of the young people had been busy all night creating enormous silhouettes, in black, of the three women in jail. Mounted at the top of the bridge in the mist and drizzle, they watched over us as we waited, lining up for coffee, singing Granny songs, trying to keep warm and shivering with more than cold. The trees loomed around as if to protect us, and a lone drummer echoed the beating of our hearts. It took a long time for the RCMP and the man from MacBlo to drive up and read us the injunction against blocking the road. If we didn't want to get arrested, we should move aside.

Ria and Alison sat down, along with 15 others. The singing changed, quieter now, more like prayers to the Earth. Even the drum was silent as we heard the trucks coming, bringing the loggers. Not many of them, fewer than a dozen. They stopped behind the RCMP cars and the school bus chartered to take us to jail.

Alison got out her knitting and Sergeant Len Doyle, the arresting officer, came over to make sure we had read the injunction and would not move off. It all seemed like a play: the cameramen waiting, the spectators chanting, the RCMP politely performing

At the Clayoquot protest in 1993, these three cutouts stood guard on the Kennedy Lake Road bridge. The cutouts were of three women then in jail for defying a court injunction against the protest.

their routine roles. Ria and Alison considered going limp so they would have to be carried, but were nervous about showing their underwear and went quietly, walking to the bus, where Sergeant Doyle took away Alison's knitting — very dangerous stuff.

When the bus left with a full complement of protesters, everybody cheered, but when the loggers drove over the black cardboard cut-outs of the three women in jail, the tears flowed. In custody at the Ucluelet RCMP detachment, Alison and Ria sang in their holding cell, which may have speeded up the process of identifying, fingerprinting and photographing, and the promise to appear in court. The charge of criminal contempt of court for defying an injunction still seemed somewhat metaphysical. All they had done was sit on a very wet road.

Ria (looking up) and Alison (knitting) are served notices of injunction as they sit on Kennedy Lake Road at Clayoquot.

Sergeant Doyle gave Alison back her knitting, with not a stitch dropped. (While awaiting trial the following year, she knitted him a pair of multicoloured socks.) Ria and Alison were released the same day to the others who were waiting outside and we celebrated in true Granny fashion by going to lunch at the restaurant in the Wickaninnish tourist centre near Long Beach, where Anita explained to our waiter how to make tea and Ria announced that if we were any more trouble she'd take us back to the nursing home. We were all a little hyper from our criminal activities.

That was a busy fall. Ria and Alison accompanied a busload of nervous church people who wanted to join the protest but needed to know what to expect. Later we all went up to Clayoquot for Inger to have her turn; we cheered her on and picked her up at the

RCMP detachment in Ucluelet. Winter rains began and the camp closed. More than 900 people had been arrested. What would they do with us all? There was talk of mass trials in a downtown theatre. Many of us worked at the resource centre set up in a donated office in Victoria, sorting out names and addresses and finding free lawyers and billets for out-of-town defendants. Worried parents called from afar. Betty tried to make a master list, but who was "Rainbow" or "Star Child"? We looked for lawyers and signed up witnesses to attend the trials but nobody seriously contemplated jail sentences.

Young women in white dresses, with flowers in their hair, sat stunned as they encountered the intricacies of the justice system. The lawyers we had signed up changed their minds because of time constraints. There would be no adjournments and no time for defendants to do their own research in the law library, since it was only open when they had to be in court. One 17-year-old insisted on his right to be in school instead of court and was arrested in school and jailed. Denied the right to call witnesses, defendants were reduced to reciting Dr. Seuss's animal fable *The Lorax* or citing Socrates, Chief Seattle, Oscar Wilde, Buddha and Jesus. While awaiting sentence, dozens danced round the courthouse, holding hands. When Judge John Bouck handed down sentences of 45 to 60 days in jail and a fine of $1,000 to each of the first 45 defendants, everyone gasped.

All through that winter and well into the spring of 1994, Grannies sat with defendants as different judges handed out wildly different sentences, from probation to six months in jail. Judge Alan Low, recycled for a second stint on the bench, announced, "I've heard it all and I'm tired of hearing about trees."

It was January 1994 when Alison got her turn in court, wearing a very plain Granny hat in case it offended Judge Kenneth MacKenzie. It sprouted more flowers each day. Convicted, she insisted that "the Raging Grannies do not apologize. We stand up — or sit down — for our beliefs." So it was a $500 fine and 21 days in jail, with the offer of house arrest with an electronic ankle bracelet to monitor her movements. Jail sounded much more interesting — and it was.

Brannen Lake Correctional Centre outside Nanaimo was Canada's only co-ed jail. The handful of female protesters joined more than 200 male offenders, who went bug-eyed over the long-haired girls sharing free time with them every evening, and appeared to see Alison as a mother confessor, bending her ear with boasts about their wickedness or insistence that they had been framed. They all seemed the most unsuccessful criminals. Alison got out of kitchen duty the second day by slicing her thumb on the meat-cutting machine, which added considerable protein to the breakfast and much increased her standing as a quick study in the art of malingering. She spent her time trying to organize a library strong on thrillers, and teaching English to a Vietnamese drug dealer who has probably profited immensely and may now be an international tycoon.

She found her fellow female detainees just as interesting: very young, very defiant but a little scared, deep into Tarot cards and totems and big on beads. They did a lot of yoga and hugging. And they all got into trouble for making friends with Fluffy, the Rottweiler dog kennelled close to their dormitory. "She's supposed to be a guard dog. Now you're spoiling her," Alison was rebuked. She also got into trouble for not fastening all the buttons on her forest-green uniform. The coveralls came in two sizes — too small and too large.

Some of the young male Clayoquot "protectors" had a hard time with other inmates, but Alison found jail very similar to her British boarding school, except that the prison food was better. And the Grannies augmented it by smuggling in chocolates, hidden in their bras, when they came to visit. She was almost sorry when she got seven days off for "good behaviour" and left early. She bought an eagle mask from Jimmy Jules, one of many First Nations inmates, with her 25-cents-an-hour earnings of $40, left behind a "camp" song for the guys, extolling "NCC, Brannen Lake, where they serve you pizza and cake," and handed in her uniform. Female inmate

8304620 was free to go and the Grannies were waiting outside, where, said the guards, they'd been making rather a lot of noise.

Ria opted for house arrest and community service, which she performed by making a marvellous tapestry of the Clayoquot rainforest for Transition House, a women's shelter in Victoria. Merve and Anne Wilkinson, who had been arrested at another "seniors' special" and were representing themselves in court, were lauded by their judge for being "magnificently unrepentant" and were able to claim their normal lives as time served for community service. Inger got the worst treatment of all, because by the time she was sentenced to jail, no more women protesters were being sent to the Nanaimo "country club." It must have been Alison's friendship with Fluffy that cancelled its co-ed status. Inger was driven off in a paddy wagon, stuck in it on the car deck for the ferry crossing to Vancouver and then transported to the Burnaby Correctional Centre for Women. There she shared a "cottage" with some Doukhobor women whose vegetarian cooking was much better than the canteen's and whose stories of burning down their homes to protest laws that offended their religion reminded her that civil disobedience has a long and important tradition in Canada.

Meanwhile, protests against the trials and sentences poured in from around the world. Three U.S. congressmen pressed Vice-President Al Gore to "do something." Canadian writers and lawyers weighed in. Robert Kennedy Jr., an environmental lawyer with the Natural Resources Defence Council in Washington, D.C., added his voice. The Canadian Ambassador to the UN for the Environment, Arthur Campeau, claimed that Clayoquot was making Canada look like "an environmental outlaw" and *The Globe and Mail* reported results of a B.C. poll: 81 percent blamed the War in the Woods on poor logging practices and 62 percent were in favour of asking the UN to supervise logging in B.C. MacBlo made a last push, launching conspiracy charges against Tzeporah Berman, the charismatic young woman who had been camp leader but who had never once blocked the road. Those charges were dismissed, but so were a number of appeals against Clayoquot convictions. Svend Robinson, an NDP MP, had to remind the authorities that charges against him for joining the blockade had never been processed. So he went to jail for 14 days and insisted that his pay as an MP be docked for time served.

We keep on bumping into the folk we met at Clayoquot. We hug a lot. There was a five-year reunion in 1998 on an island in the sound, where it was somewhat startling to find that one scruffy teenager had now become a lawyer and others had "put on suits" without losing their convictions. Alison found herself walking in the following year's Earth Walk in Victoria beside the guard who had booked her into Victoria's Wilkinson Road Jail before she was taken to Nanaimo. He said he'd learned a lot since then, and so had we all. By the time we met for the 10th anniversary in 2003 we were convinced it was a battle we had won, because Clayoquot Sound had become a UN biosphere reserve in 2000 and agreements had been signed between some of the First Nations and the logging companies. The Friends of Clayoquot Sound continue to keep their watchdog position, however, chasing after companies that gnaw at the edges of the protected areas. Weyerhaeuser, a multinational corporation, bought MacMillan Bloedel for $3.5 billion in 1999, but we think it is no more environmentally friendly than MacBlo.

The battle didn't just save Clayoquot: It lifted the whole environmental movement onto the front pages and brought massive awareness of our planet's fragility. It also gave rise to even wider protest movements and acceptance of the idea that civil disobedience might be necessary if governments fail in their responsibilities. When 900 people sat down on that road in 1993, they sowed the seeds of mass protests that led to the APEC clash in Vancouver in 1998, the Battle in Seattle in 1999 and large demonstrations in Quebec in 2001 and Calgary in 2002.

The Grannies changed too. We'd won the respect of hundreds of younger folk and we'd conquered any remaining fears of authority. We weren't planning a career of crime, but there'd be no stopping us now if a sit-down was necessary.

FISHES

Sung to the tune of "Three Little Fishes,"
traditional; lyrics by Alison Acker

Out in the ocean in a nice polluted sea
Swam a school of fishes, as happy as can be.
We're going back to Canada, where we all began.
But, wait a minute, fishes, they've got another plan.

Chorus: Boop, boop. diddum, daddum, waddum, choo [x 3]
'cos you'll never make it back up to the river to spawn.

What happened to the turbot, the herring and the cod
Is happening to the salmon, and don't blame it all on God.
Greedy politicians can squabble through the night
But we won't give up our salmon without a good fight.

Chorus: Boop, boop, diddum, daddum, waddum, choo.
Boop, boop, diddum, daddum, waddum, choo
Boop, boop, diddum, we need another plan
And we know we can't rely on David Anderson.*

*Federal minister for the environment from Victoria.

GOING GREEN WITH STYLE

I could not at any age be content to take my place in a corner by the fireplace and simply look on.
— *Eleanor Roosevelt*

The War in the Woods brought in fresh recruits, and we sure needed them. Maryanne Campeau was to be our youngest Granny, in her 40s when she joined. As a teenager in Brockville, Ontario, she volunteered at a psychiatric hospital, worked for the NDP and organized a local chapter of Oxfam. Her Grade 11 teacher arranged a peaceful demonstration at the U.S. border against weapons testing, and by whining and pleading with her parents she got permission to go along. She trained as a counsellor for people with developmental disabilities, but decided instead to head for the Cariboo in B.C. and live on a trapline by herself. When she got to her new "home" she found a tiny log cabin with a dirt floor, half a roof, no door and extra-small windows to discourage bears, but she stuck it out all winter.

Coming south to Victoria, she continued to work with children with special needs and also started a study of medicinal herbs. Her son, Caleb, born in 1989, made the local paper when he was photographed carrying a peace sign during the Gulf War and he was with her when she was arrested at Clayoquot. Because she was a single mother she didn't go to jail but had to do community service. It was at Clayoquot that she met us and we were lucky to get her, since she already had the knowledge we'd been struggling to acquire about all the bad things spoiling our environment and our bodies.

Unfortunately, Maryanne's chronic renal failure has limited her activities with the Grannies. We love it when she comes to rallies with us because she is great at heckling the provincial Liberal government. She does as much as she can and we know it is an emotional struggle for her to accept her physical limitations. As the rest of us get creakier, we can learn a lot from Maryanne.

Joyce Lee was a godsend because she, also, was well educated in natural science. She was an ardent organizer for the protection of the Garry oak, southern Vancouver Island's endangered tree. A gnarled affair that looks as if it came straight out of the Tolkien trilogy and always seems on the point of death, the Garry oak is nevertheless a Victoria icon and you injure it at your peril. A lot of local developers didn't seem to care, but Joyce and her cohorts did. She turned us on to local threats to our environment, and we were sorry to see her go to the mainland and back to university.

Doreen Wood was feeling very down about hopes for peace until she found the Grannies. Her horror of war comes from direct experience: she was aboard HMS Excellent, a naval shore establishment on Whale Island just off Portsmouth Dockyard in England during World War II, when sailors returned from trying to pluck the British Expeditionary Force off the beaches at Dunkirk. She had to record their experiences and is still haunted by the memories.

In Montreal, when she was giving birth to her first son, she ended up in a gynecological ward where most of the other patients were experiencing the aftermath of messed-up abortions. Some had borne up to 15 children and had been only 14 or 15 years old when they got married. That led to her passionate engagement in the abortion issue and in the fight for women's rights. Unfortunately, failing health has kept her away from Granny activities recently, but she loves hearing what we do and wishes she could do more.

Several other Grannies signed up around this time but had to leave. Grace Tickson joined and then moved up Vancouver Island, where she is strongly involved in the same causes today. Connie Wright was with us briefly, but she died shortly afterward, from cancer.

Being a Granny is indeed a lot of work. We say it keeps us healthy, but it certainly isn't for everyone. Granny Alice Coppard, with the Vancouver gaggle, kept up her Grannying well into her 90s. At her 90th birthday party, the husband of one of the Grannies presented and fitted her with a scarlet garter. Other gaggles also cherish Grannies of equal experience. Our philosophy seems to be that we don't have all that much time left to change the world, so we'd better get on with it.

In 1993, we were brassy enough to go blonde. That was the year B.C.'s Kim Campbell became the first woman prime minister of Canada. She got the job after Brian Mulroney resigned, hoping that his departure might make the Progressive Conservative Party more acceptable to Canadian voters. Campbell's tenure lasted just four months. The PCs went down to defeat in the election that same year, slashed from 155 seats in the House of Commons to two, and Campbell lost her Vancouver seat.

Grannies, of course, weren't very fond of the Progressive Conservatives, whether male or female, given their espousal of free trade, federal squabbles with Quebec, the prospect of expensive helicopter acquisitions and the emerging Somalia scandal about rogue troops torturing a boy to death. The media were cruel to Campbell, and so were we. A photograph of her holding her lawyer's gown in front of her naked shoulders appeared in a book of portraits and then in the media. If she could bare it, so could we.

At a Conservative Party meeting in a church hall in Victoria, we decided to pre-empt the speaker. The organizers didn't like the idea one bit, but faced with eight Grannies dressed in legal gowns and blonde wigs, they were helpless. We simply pushed forward and took over. It's a style of operation we have copied ever since, finding that a couple of guys on security duty can't physically stop a herd of Grannies. Our blonde wigs came from local secondhand stores (we were assured they held no lice, though we sprayed to make sure). Dressed in black, we contrived to bare our left shoulders — none as luscious as Kim's, but then we weren't 46 years old anymore either. We even had a Kim song, hailing her as "the Madonna of the west, Maggie Thatcher's little sister, Joan of Arc, but better dressed, Boadicea with a smile, Ghengis Khan but with more style." The audience was stunned. Campbell was later to comment: "A comparison between Madonna and me is a comparison between a strapless evening gown and a gownless evening strap." We are still trying to sort out what she meant.

The "Kimette" experience led some of us into more adventurous attire. Other Granny gaggles opt for aprons and bonnets or Granny T-shirts, with an image of a row of Grannies' bottoms and the message: "More widespread than ever." We did at one time adopt pink running shoes and most of us sport feather boas, but we don't like to look alike, probably because we are such individualists. In fact, once we had a Granny in army boots and black leather who did indeed ride a Harley, though she didn't stay with us long. But it was a trip to Port Angeles that opened our eyes to more fashion possibilities.

In 1995 we were invited to take part in a spring festival in Port Angeles, Washington, just across the Strait of Juan de Fuca. Checking into our motel, we found to our surprise that we were not the only oddballs in town. At first, when we read the group's leaflets, we thought this other strange bunch was all fired up by some sort of discrimination. And they were. We soon realized, however, that the motel had housed us with a gathering of transvestites.

These men who like to dress in women's clothing had come from all over the continent for a weekend conference. We wondered if the motel management had mixed us up and thought we were transvestites too. We thought this hilarious and were soon in whoops of laughter. We kept the doors half open so we could peek out unobtrusively, being rewarded by intriguing glimpses of men in stylish fashions, gorgeous wigs and impeccable makeup.

One guy was garbed in shades of mauve and purple. Being over six feet tall, he was very grand and imposing, but he did have a very long waist.

Next morning we hurried along to breakfast, eager to see more, but the waitress told us that 30 of them had left on the morning ferry to take tea at Victoria's venerable Empress Hotel. We would have liked to see that. We tried not to stare at the remaining members in the dining room, but couldn't help a few glances. These guys were *Vogue* magazine's version of women dressed to the nines. They sat the way women sit round a table. Nylon-covered shaved legs were decorously crossed. Shoes were large but stylish, mostly colourful, low-heeled pumps. Pinkies were raised above china coffee cups as they leaned forward to chat cozily with each other. Their hats were to die for.

We got dressed for our gig. The usual: pink socks and runners, red feathers, tired flowery hats, thrift-shop dresses — a definite letdown compared to these men. When we ran into them in the hall, we introduced ourselves and chatted with them about our dressing up as Raging Grannies. We found ourselves thinking they were women, like us, because they acted like women, with a woman's way of polite curiosity about who we were and what we were up to. They had better manners than we were showing in our nosiness. We had been surreptitiously examining their faces for whiskers and wondering if their voices were real or assumed. They, on the other hand, were simply being friendly, even gracious. We felt ashamed of our voyeurism.

A couple of them said they would come to our gig, and Granny Doreen reported on a genuine heart-to-heart chat on the way there when she hitched a ride in a stunning, silver-grey Mercedes. We did our gig at the local recreation centre, lined up for the ferry and forgot all about the transvestites until we noticed them disembarking from the vessel after their tea at the Empress. Two by two or in groups of three, they glided down the long gangway in their pumps, though their feet must have been killing them. Betty had acquired a blister and could sympathize.

We must confess we giggled quietly and unobtrusively — we hope — as we assessed each perfect costume. They wore the sort of raiment most of us had worn in the days before women were liberated from corsets and high heels and the pressure to aim for *haute couture*. Remember when women in pantsuits weren't allowed into classy places, such as the Union Club in Victoria? How times have changed. Men in drag taking tea at the Empress. Did they gossip together over cucumber sandwiches, strawberries and Darjeeling?

We weren't the only ones aware of the male beauties coming off the boat. "Hey, there's another one of the faggots." A pack of macho teenagers was clearly intent on taunting these male anomalies. Separated from the returning transvestites by a ceiling-high, chain-link fence, these guys in sweaty T-shirts and back-to-front baseball caps obviously felt safe to guffaw and make rude gestures as each tired traveller passed.

Astonished at herself, Betty got to her feet, shouting, "Stop it. You guys, stop that. Stop that right now. Stop being so awful." All the other Grannies rose to their feet, raging like Betty. Imagine thinking we could take on these teens. But why be Raging Grannies if we had no spunk? Besides, if we had the chutzpah to take on the U.S. Navy, these punks were nothing. We must have looked pretty fierce because the hazing stopped.

"My goodness," said Betty, slightly bewildered. "I'm not quite sure what I'm defending here."

"Their right to be different," suggested Alison.

"Other human beings with lots of courage," said Mary.

But maybe there's another perspective. Once women put on pants we never looked back. Does it follow that if macho men start wearing dresses, it's a fast-forward to the end of patriarchy? And an end to those erotic, macho, multiple-warhead Trident submarines? Wouldn't that be something to celebrate?

The 1990s were rapidly revealing to us the precarious state of the world around us. Gasoline-guzzling cars were polluting the atmosphere and causing global warming. The fish were dying.

So were the butterflies. Who knows what would be next? The Grannies had to take a stand.

We took up a popular environmental cause to prevent further pollution from cars, namely the preservation of the Esquimalt & Nanaimo Railway, threatened with shutdown in 1987, again in 1994 and in 2001. To this day its fate is still uncertain. With our somewhat convoluted logic, the Grannies decided to protest in 1994 by stopping the train to deliver a Valentine Day's card to the engineer.

The E & N isn't one of those big transcontinental trains. It's a once-a-day affair, more or less on schedule, with from one to three Budd diesel cars, hard seats and no food service. It's slow, but for years it has been the transport of choice for many Victorians going up Vancouver Island as far as Courtenay or up-island residents coming down to the big city. It's a friendly affair, with a ticket taker who collects railroad badges and loves to chat with passengers. The train stops for bears or wayward cows that wander onto the track. Occasionally it runs out of whatever keeps it going, or maybe something falls off. Anyway, passengers sometimes have to wait for a bus to take over and get them to their destination.

Nevertheless, many Victorians are madly in love with their train, and environmentalists rejoice because it is so much less polluting than road traffic. The E & N once carried coal and lumber; it still takes children to see their grannies and tourists to gape at the wonderful views from high trestle bridges spanning ravines.

Since it is highly illegal to stop a train, even "the little train that could," Anne spoke ahead of time to the engineer and advised him of our intentions. Apparently she got his agreement that he would stop for two or three minutes at the designated spot at Nanoose Bay. After all, we wouldn't create much more "down time" than a stubborn cow on the tracks. Anne also arranged local radio and TV coverage and a gathering of about 60 protesters. We wanted it to stop at Nanoose so that we could link the train issue with the rankling problem of the U.S. nuclear submarines visiting the Nanoose test site.

We do our bit in 1994 to try and save the Esquimalt & Nanaimo Railway. Robyn Smith, a Vancouver Granny, is at the right end of the banner.

Also, the province was looking at various possible sites for a new ferry terminal on Vancouver Island. If it was built at Nanoose, that should neatly get rid of the submarines and encourage tourists arriving on B.C. ferries to board the train and go north to Courtenay or south to Victoria. And it would stimulate the economy. Grannies think of everything.

So, at 11:30 A.M. in the rain, Grannies in damp feathers and finery joined local citizens to scramble down the railway embankment and line up along the tracks to stop the train, much as Bill Miner, the Grey Fox, waited along mainland tracks to hold up trains and grab the loot.

Alison presented the card and flowers to the engineer. We blew him kisses, the CHEK-TV cameras did their thing, some of us said a few words, and it was done. We had held up our first train. But we hadn't saved it, nor had we gotten rid of the subs, because the new ferry terminal was built farther south, at Nanaimo.

Eight years later, the powers that be demonstrated their imperviousness to Granny advice. The E & N was again threatened with shutdown, so a dozen Grannies boarded the train on what was rumoured to be one of its last runs. We hoped to persuade B.C.'s minister of transport, Judith Reid, that the E & N had to be saved. She, of course, had been called away from her office in Parksville when we arrived, after a two-kilometre hike from the train station. We got more satisfaction from our lunch than from her assistant.

We gathered two more times at the E & N station in Victoria to support local attempts to keep the train running. We sang Jane's song "O Give Me A Train," which goes back to our early efforts in 1987, showing how little things had changed. Maybe we touched somebody's conscience or good sense, because as of 2004 we still have our E & N, although it has only one coach some days, and there still isn't any food aboard.

A U.S. tour company did operate short trips from Victoria to an upscale resort on top of the Malahat, but it didn't make money and closed after a year. Nobody seemed to want to invest in the E & N, though we see it as a tremendous tourist asset. We'd love to have an old-fashioned steam engine and we might even get to blow the whistle. And maybe we will. At last, a group of investors formed the Vancouver Island Railway Company in March 2003, offering a deal to the present owner, Rail America, that would keep both freight and passenger service open. We can't wait.

About this time Anita launched her toilet-paper campaign. Greenpeace had convinced her that chlorine devastates our environment and almost all the toilet paper available in Victoria was bleached with chlorine, except for a brand named Seventh Generation, nice and whitish, no chlorine, and we're not quite sure what it's made of. So Anita began checking up on the YM-YWCA, the B.C. legislature, the Anglican Cathedral and other offices and stores to find out who was using the bad, bleached stuff and needed a lecture. Those who listened got a free, four-roll package of the good kind and a few lines of our Raging Granny song that proclaims, "Whether standing up or sitting, it is absolutely fitting, we decide to stop committing environmental crime." (We do try to include men, too.)

In June 1992 we expressed our displeasure by singing, "The Water's More Sour Than Wine" to the Capital Regional District water board because it allowed logging in Victoria's watershed. Logging was ruining the taste of our drinking water. Tourists were noticing.

Alison's song was duly entered into the public record and hey, we did look angelic in the *Times Colonist* photo!

> Drink to me only with thine eyes
> For water we must decline.
> Don't trust that tap
> Or fill up that glass,
> The water's more sour than wine.
>
> It may come from rain,
> But we must abstain.
> Who knows where it's been since then.
> One thing for sure,
> It can't still be pure
> If they're logging Sooke Lake again.

In August 1992 we linked up with the Action Canada Network, a loose coalition against free trade with the United States for a demonstration at Victoria's main intersection — Douglas and Yates. Fran, dressed as Uncle Sam in a star-spangled hat, flipped a pathetic but patriotic toy beaver in a frying pan to demonstrate what we thought free trade was doing to Canada. Alison, Fran and Betty sang Alison's "Unity Song" to the tune of "My Bonnie Lies Over the Ocean" for the CHEK-TV cameraman:

> We love our Canadian beaver.
> He's one of those endangered types.

We don't want him fried by Mulroney
Or covered in spangles and stripes.

Our environmental conscience, honed by our exertions to save Clayoquot Sound from the logging companies, began to explode everywhere, due in part to Maryanne and Joyce. They were intent on saving Mother Earth, though sometimes it seemed like sieving the sea.

Our attention turned now to salmon. The breakdown of the Pacific Salmon Treaty between Canada and the U.S. in 1993 and a drop in our salmon stocks focused us on Ayum Creek in Sooke, a salmon stream right next to Maryanne's home. Its banks were scheduled to be clear-cut by a developer. Maryanne and Freda Knott, who also lives close by, joined the campaign to save the creek and persuaded us to help.

Freda came to the Grannies as a well-loved friend. We knew her from the Greater Victoria Disarmament Group, where she toiled for many years. She was representing that group aboard the Greenpeace ship *Rainbow Warrior II* with us when we sailed to Ketchikan, Alaska, to protest nuclear ships passing through Canadian waters to reach Dixon Entrance.

Freda grew up in a progressive Jewish home in Vancouver. Both parents were active in peace and left-wing movements, and she remembers accompanying them to collect signatures on the street corner for the Ban the Bomb Petition, which eventually contained six million names worldwide. When she decided to join us she was despairing of the new world order. Having been a Communist most of her life, she saw the USSR she had once admired crumbling into moral, social and economic chaos, and Western capitalism didn't seem like any alternative. In the beginning, though, she was not a Granny fan.

"My first impression, being a rather cautious person, was that dressing in outrageous clothing and acting as they did would be insulting to many older women. However, I saw the very warm reception they received and realized that they were playing a very important role in bringing social and peace issues to the public at large," she says, adding, "Besides, it was time to bring some humour into my activism." Now she says, "The Grannies have become very dear to me. They're my friends and confidantes. They have helped to make my life meaningful and enjoyable."

Freda was married to Erni, 18 years her senior, a former logger and member of the Industrial Workers of the World (Wobblies) and a Communist Party federal candidate. Until his death in December 2003, Erni had a large market garden and kept bees, so they both spent Sundays selling produce at the Metchosin Farmers' Market near Victoria. As if she weren't busy enough, Freda is also a board member of the Victoria chapter of the Council of Canadians and a leading organizer of Victoria's annual Earth Walk. (It started out as a peace walk, morphed into a walk for the environment and is now a walk for global justice.) She's one of our smallest Grannies and the bounciest. We love it when she gets excited and stamps her feet on stage to protest whatever ills are threatening us. Freda is a very active member of the Victoria Solidarity Coalition, which many local activists consider to be the unofficial opposition to the B.C. Liberal government. (The 2001 NDP electoral rout meant there were only two NDP members, both of them women, confronting the Liberal agenda in the legislature.)

With Freda and Maryanne whipping us into shape, we joined a protest at Ayum Creek organized by Metchosin's Joanne Manley. Alongside a host of young people wearing salmon heads as hats, we tramped beside the endangered creek bed to the ocean. We sang our fishy song, "Boop-Boop-a-Diddum," to warn all those poor little fishes about the big trawlers offshore and developers and logging companies messing up their spawning grounds on land. It was great to see school kids take up the message, learning how to be streamkeepers and how to bother politicians. And this time the protest succeeded. Ayum Creek was saved. It became a protected area and the salmon returned in great numbers. We like to think we played a small part.

Cows came next, and weren't so easy to deal with. What worried us was not cow extinction, but the growing use of bovine growth hormone (BGH), administered to cows to increase their yield of milk, and a very possible cause of an increase in cancerous tumours in humans. Besides, we were convinced it wasn't good for cows. Canada's one-year moratorium on the use of BGH was due to expire in 1997, and we wanted assurances from local dairies that they would not use it. The maker of BGH was Monsanto — a name we were to hear more of in the years ahead. Island Farms Dairies Co-op Association had its head office on Blanshard Street in Victoria, a main artery leading out of town, so that's where we gathered, along with some stuffed cows and supplies of milk and cookies for passersby. Inger wore her Viking helmet with horns. Since we'd learned that BGH made cows prone to painfully swollen hind legs, those of us with varicose veins sympathized, so some of us also sported "udders" — inflated rubber gloves — claiming, in jest, that we cows were "udderly" excited about the new hormone in spite of its side effects. (There are no depths to which we will not sink for a pun.)

With the late Derek Mallard and his wife, Gwen, of the Citizens Association to Save the Environment, we pursued Island Farms officials to their offices, pointing out that BGH had been banned in much of the world already. And, again, the battle was won. We can't claim that our gentle mooing scared off Monsanto, but the moratorium has stayed in effect at our local dairies and the Grannies moved on to save something else.

It was the turn of the endangered Garry oak, the one that always looks on the point of death. Joyce persuaded us it would live forever if we could keep the developers away. We added oak trees to our list of causes and on we went. Soon we were campaigning for the marbled murrelet, the Vancouver Island marmot, the grizzly bear and the monarch butterfly, which was threatened by aerial spraying against the gypsy moth. Alison and Betty even spent an afternoon getting covered with glue, making gypsy-moth traps that were far more environmentally sound

Betty, Alison and Maryanne (left to right) demonstrate our "udder" opposition to the use of bovine growth hormone at Island Farms Dairies in Victoria. (RAY SMITH/VICTORIA *TIMES COLONIST* PHOTO)

than aerial spraying, we were told, but only if folded properly, which was a skill we sadly lacked. Some Grannies threatened to collapse themselves under the weight of so many threats to the environment. But where to draw the line? It was often an individual Granny, impelled to action by a local threat, who pulled us all in.

In 1998, Betty and Alison discovered that the lovely hill behind their Esquimalt homes was due for development. Since Garry oaks rambled over those slopes, which comprised the last untouched land overlooking Victoria Harbour, this was surely a Granny issue. Led by Betty, we inflated balloons to show how high the proposed high-rise buildings would go and leafletted pedestrians on the Westsong Walkway that runs below the hill to the city. There were noisy civic meetings, leading to the developers being turned down. Other developers tried again, and then backed off. As of this writing, the area, known as the Matson Lands, is still undeveloped, though there is a more benign plan being considered that would see development on the crest of the hill with protection for the precious Garry oak meadow below.

Next came Freda's turn. The Royal Bay development in Metchosin threatened land where Emily Carr had once painted treetops soaring to the sky. The Grannies weighed in with songs at a protest meeting, but this time the development went ahead. Even our lament to the ghost of Emily Carr couldn't win that one. Win some, lose some. Freda's next urging came when the owner of a local woodlot threatened to turn it into a gravel pit. We sang again at a protest, and so far, the threats have remained only threats.

A much wider concern, and the first thing many tourists point out, is Victoria's practice of emptying our raw sewage into the ocean. Experts insist that our swirling currents and high tides dissipate anything toxic, but the sight of gulls massing around the outflow to snatch the fish that thrive on our sewage does tend to upset weak stomachs. Whether for or against a change in our sewage treatment, audiences seem to love our song that proclaims satirically: "Victorians produce it odour free."

And as for all the nasties that accumulate on our shores, the Grannies have led the campaign to clean up the beaches. Anxious to prove we practise what we preach, we have annually stomped up and down beaches with garbage bags, picking up our share of condoms, bottles and obscure tangles of wire. Our song about such treasure became adopted as a beach-clean-up ditty even south of the border, appearing in the International Coastal Cleanup Report published by the Center for Marine Conservation in Washington, D.C. We felt righteous and rewarded, but we were soon to face a health and environmental threat of staggering proportions — genetic engineering.

We're not sure how our awareness grew. It was probably the food purists among us, the ones who buy only organic, who brought the news that genetically modified foods were invading our supermarkets. Was there no way to stop them?

We read in horror about Monsanto's manufacture of Terminator seeds, which meant that farmers could no longer save seeds from their own crops but had to buy them every year from the biotech companies. Soon most of the world, except the U.S., was united against the corporation that had made farmers everywhere the slaves of biotech production by forcing them to buy genetically modified seed. We wanted our government to ban any foodstuffs produced by genetic engineering, which meant corn, potatoes, soybeans, tomatoes and canola — a highly important crop for prairie farmers and the oil used in most fast foods. By 1999, the campaign against genetically modified organisms (GMOs) was Canada-wide. There was even a provincial inquiry brewing, conducted by the B.C. Legislative Assembly's Select Standing Committee on Agriculture and Fisheries. We appeared before the committee and Fran read them a convincing argument that we should do more than label food containing GMOs; we should ban it. Then we all sang "The Chemical Restaurant" song that we had borrowed from the Salt Spring Island Grannies and made sure every word went into Hansard. One of the nicest surprises was to hear a very thoroughly researched submission from the Women's Institute. We weren't the only women's group who'd had to go back to Chemistry 101.

For the next few years we lobbied local supermarket suppliers, wrote to MPs and the government and took part in rallies alongside protesters dressed as tomato-fish, one of Monsanto's brightest experiments, which involved adding fish genes to tomatoes. We got a list of all the organic producers on Vancouver Island and vowed to use their products wherever possible, knowing that the organic label guaranteed no genetic engineering, though not all non-GM food is organic.

We decided to take on the supermarkets. Some of us joined in pasting warning stickers on such stuff as canola margarine, which we knew to be genetically modified. Managers were getting wary as the protest grew, and we thought the Grannies should be educational rather than confrontational. One Friday evening in November 1999, three Grannies filled their shopping baskets with carefully selected items and headed for the checkout counter with the longest line. There, Fran hesitated and asked, "Do you know if this is made from genetically modified corn?" The clerk had to endure an education. Next item, tomato sauce, and the same routine. Then potatoes. Then soy sauce. By now another clerk was involved as Inger began to unload her basket in another line, pose the same questions and start the educational process. Then came Mary. This time the clerk phoned the manager to ask him the same questions. When he said that all the products involved were probably genetically modified, one of the clerks asked, "Then why aren't these things labelled?" Indeed, why not?

We encouraged clerks and customers in the store to write to David Anderson, Canada's minister of the environment and the only cabinet minister with a seat in Victoria, and then we left quietly. Chipping away at a problem might not change things overnight, but if everybody did it, we'd win the battle. But of course we didn't win. The Canadian government still hasn't banned GM food or insisted on labelling it as such, but we are delighted that our European cousins now have a law requiring producers to label any products containing more than 0.9 percent genetically modified organisms.

Who cares about genetically modified food? More than just a few Grannies in Victoria. An ABC-TV news poll in June 2001 showed that 94 percent of U.S. respondents wanted labels to indicate what had been modified, and 57 percent said they'd be less likely to buy such food if they'd seen the label. Around the world, pressure against GM foods is much more intense and better organized, with 35 nations, representing a billion people, demanding or working on mandatory labelling. Ottawa is still dawdling, despite polls that show 90 percent of Canadians want labelling.

Against governments there is enormous pressure from the Gene Giants — Monsanto, Upjohn, Dow, Dupont, etc. — threatening to use the World Trade Organization to take action against countries banning their products. The companies launched a $60-million-a-year public-relations campaign to calm consumers' fears. They are desperate because both U.S. and Canadian farm exports have fallen hard since overseas buyers started rejecting the biotech crops that came on the market in 1996. The consumer lobby in North America is also starting to gain strength. While many people would prefer an outright ban on GMOs, labelling is a good start. As Norman Braksick, president of Asgrow Seed Company (now owned by Monsanto), predicted in 1994, "If you put a label on a genetically engineered food, you might as well put a skull and crossbones on it." Exactly!

As for industry propaganda, polls show that the more consumers hear about GMOs, the more resistant they become, whether the news is of protests and threats to health or even cozy commercials put out by the Gene Giants.

To become better informed and to ask embarrassing questions, in April 2001 we attended an information session with the spokesman for Thrifty Foods. It's the locally owned supermarket we all like best because it is generous to local worthy causes and its produce is so good. The information session was held at a seniors' centre and we went in civvies, trying to blend in. We weren't the only people in the audience to leave in disappointment. We'd asked all the nasty questions and found out that not even Thrifty's could stop the spread of GM foods. Almost all the canned or frozen food they sold contained some GMOs.

And the food industry was not united in pushing for labelling. It was all part of globalization: the power of corporations to run our lives, endanger our health, threaten the environment and make themselves rich at our expense. This was bigger than tomato-fish.

Sometimes, it's hard to see our progress in making the world a better place.

GRANNY GENES

Sung to the tune of "The Frozen Logger,"
by James Stevens, 1927; lyrics by Alison Acker

Now they're cloning sheep and piggies
And feeding pork to beans,
Maybe it's time for Grannies
To auction off their genes.

Our joints are kinda creaky.
Our livers are passé.
The rest is kinda leaky
But we've still got DNA.

We're not sure where to find it,
But we're told it's quite unique.
If genetic pirates want it
They'll have to play hide and seek.

Better still, let's veto
A science that's not benign.
Do they know what they are doing?
Remember Frankenstein.

WAVING THE FLAG

Well-behaved women rarely make history.
— *Laurel Thatcher Ulrich*

Some of our victories have, indeed, been small, but we have had them. Early in our Grannying days we became incensed about the spread of pornography in our fair city. We stood outside the newly opened Red Hot Video store in Esquimalt, hoping to intimidate would-be customers by brandishing a camera. The police, who were two minutes away, took 30 minutes to respond to the owners' request to move us along. The municipality of Esquimalt did not have legal cause to close down the business, but it did have legal authority to order its relocation to the industrial area. However, its new home would be too close to the local high school. Public pressure finally ran the business out of town and we're not one bit sorry.

We also sprang into action in 1997 when a sex shop near Victoria's city hall applied to open up video booths. We appeared at city council, sang our protest song, and the application ended up in the wastebasket. It is so nice to be seen as standing up for decency.

The Grannies made our finest stand for gay rights in 1997, when an anti-gay pressure group tried to take "offending" books out of B.C. classrooms. Kari D. Simpson of the Citizens' Research Institute and the Canadian Family Action Coalition came to Victoria in a province-wide censorship campaign, to denounce three books that represented gays as competent parents: *Angela's Mum, Belinda's Bouquet* and *One Dad, Two Dads, Brown Dad, Blue Dad.* When the school board of South Surrey, B.C., removed the books, the fight for gay rights and free speech began.

Hiding our hats, some Grannies arrived early for an open meeting at the Princess Mary Restaurant in Victoria. We were required to sign in, and we obliged with the names of assorted fairy-tale characters. Inside, behind a few irate Christians, we discovered rows of teachers supporting gay rights by flaunting pink ribbons. The hall was so packed that late Grannies and other supporters had to stay outside and shout. Inside, we listened restlessly to the anti-gay paranoia, waiting for question time, and then grabbed the mike, put on our hats and, to the tune of "Take Me Out to the Ball Game," sang our satirical response:

Nuke a gay whale for Jesus,
Straighten those who are bent.
Stop kids from reading those books in school.
All they need is the old golden rule because —

We're the folk who are normal.
All you others are ill.
We are the ones who are going to heaven
And you lot are going to hell — so there!

Amid thunderous applause, we were delighted to hear the speaker say, "I'm so glad that you came out tonight." We doubt she intended that double meaning. She needed the police to escort her safely out of the hall.

In 1998 the B.C. Supreme Court concluded that the school board was wrong to ban the books. An appeal was successful, but the case went to the Supreme Court of Canada in 2002 and the school board was told to reconsider its ban. We are still waiting.

We try to be ethnically conscious, although we have not yet attracted a "Granny of colour" in Victoria. We even learned enough Inuktitut to sing a translated version of "The More We Are Together" to a national conference of more than 200 professional mediators at the Fairmont Empress Hotel in Victoria. Perhaps we were sending out a message that awareness of other cultures was a necessary part of mediation. Perhaps we were only showing off. We had gotten a friend of a friend to have the song translated, and this is how it began: *"Katima neksa hoopta, neksa hoopta, neksa hoopta."* We loved the "hoopta" bit and got quite carried away.

Another of our ventures had us sitting down for the freedom of the streets. In 1998, at the behest of local businesses, Victoria city authorities moved against street people by passing a bylaw forbidding anyone to sit, kneel or lie on the sidewalk. Alerted by the Together Against Poverty Society (TAPS), we joined others at a major intersection in sitting down, kneeling down and even putting up a tent in the hope of an arrest. Lawyers had been calling, offering free services for anybody who got arrested for contravening a bylaw that was obviously unenforceable, since it related to body position rather than any act. Betty groaned a lot, but it wasn't raining and she couldn't think of any other excuse to get out of the sit-in. The cops wisely watched and pretended nothing was happening. Nobody ever got arrested and the bylaw lapsed. Since then, city council and the police have changed their minds and got tough with street people, confiscating backpacks and even dogs, and charging exorbitant fees for their return.

A much bigger issue has been the growing gap between rich and poor in a city that likes to pretend everything is beautiful. In February 1997, we decided to see for ourselves how bad things were for the homeless. We visited Streetlink, a local shelter, learning how difficult it was for the homeless to find shelter, work, food or even a washroom. We needed to know more. We distrusted the idea of "going homeless" for a night because it sounded so insensitive to blunder round the mean streets, asking homeless people silly questions. Instead, we participated in The Poverty Game, an experience organized by the TAPS. For an evening we played the part of welfare recipients and went through the hoops they have to go through every day.

TAPS volunteers corralled us into a make-believe office, where we were not allowed to talk to each other. We were given identities that included how many kids we had and any disabilities we suffered, and were then handed a measly monthly "cheque." We rolled a dice and picked up cards that indicated everyday disasters: some kid of ours had broken the landlord's window and another had lost his shoes and the baby needed a special diet and we hadn't gotten the job we'd applied for at Wal-Mart. We'd have to plead for a cash advance. Volunteers played overworked and unsympathetic social workers who were always out or at meetings and never available for us. We got more and more frustrated with the bureaucracy and unfairness of the system and decided we couldn't push for a better world without taking up the cause of those suffering from indifference right in our city.

"But we're just being patronizing because we're not suffering," one Granny objected. And it is true that we Grannies all have homes (small ones or condos or co-ops or rented apartments or even a boat at one time) and we have some sort of pension from our working lives, though none of us is rich. But the majority agreed that social justice was a Granny issue because we did not want to live in a society where the rich got richer and the poor got poorer.

So, along with a growing number of anti-poverty activists, in 1997 we helped create the first Corporate Golden Piggy Awards (a parody of the Academy Awards), which recognize and expose the greediest corporations of the past year. The "Piggies" soon turned into an annual party. With free admission to the Roxy Theatre, owned by Howie Siegel, the audience is encouraged to dress in

VICTORIA, BC

The Victoria Raging Grannies in a flotilla of 50 craft in Victoria's Inner Harbour gathered to bid farewell to Greenpeace flagship Rainbow Warrior II.

Front canoe (left to right):
Fran, Anne Pask, Betty and Alison; Mary Rose at right in 2nd canoe.

Victoria Raging Grannies launching their navy on Parliament Hill in Ottawa; Hilda in foreground, Lois, Fran, Kathy and Anne Pask in background. Photo courtesy of The Ottawa Citizen "Use of this photo does not imply support by The Ottawa Citizen of The Raging Grannies or any of their causes, political or otherwise."

The Salt Spring Island Raging Grannies, with accompanist Barrington Perry, at the 2003 Good Food Fair.

KELOWNA, BC

The Kelowna Grannies are pictured here by Okanagan Lake, singing environmental songs at a Trans-Canada relay event April 2000.

The Kelowna Raging Grannies participated in a May 2001 fundraiser for the preservation of Gellatly Nut Farm. Left to right: Shirley Fitzpatrick, Pat Grinsteed and Muriel Rosevear. Photo by Deborah Greaves..

Left to right: Linda Sampson, Sheila Moss, Pat Grinsteed, Shelagh Faa, Freda Van Stralen, Sharon Wurmann and Shirley Fitzpatrick.

NORTH OKANAGAN, BC

The North Okanagan Raging Grannies protested the use of pesticides, Canada Day 2003 in Vernon, B.C.

The Central Alberta Raging Grannies protest against the attack on Iraq at a peace march and rally organized by the Red Deer Council of Canadians.

January 2003

Banner carried by two of the Central Alberta Raging Grannies at the FTAA summit in Quebec City in 2001.

FLEECE AND TRAMPLE ALL OVER AGAIN

CENTRAL ALBERTA RAGING GRANNIES BONJOUR QUEBEC

The Central Alberta Raging Grannies presented briefs to Premier Ralph Klein and then Environment Minister Ty Lund at a rally in Red Deer put on by Friends of the West Country

Massive USS Missouri blend prestigious past and presen

Carolyn Heiman
Colonist staff

U.S. Navy battleship on which signed surrender documents the Second Wo

CALGARY, AB

June 2002

e Calgary Raging Grannies were joined by the Edmonton
gaggle for G-8 protests at Calgary Olympic Plaza

November 2002

The Calgary Raging Grannies in a
rally against sweatshops

TORONTO, ON

august 6, 2003

NO MORE HIROSHIMA

left to right: Marsha Furuya, Marty Sweet,
Joan Harvey, Kate Chung, Dee Stapleton,
Phyllis Creighton and Inge Biskupski

The Toronto Raging Grannies at the Hiroshima
Day commemoration in Toronto

May 1999

JOE
(ingle Bells)

e's back in stores agai
at Might is Right
s without Pain.
makes every fr
l solve ol
eapon ar
s will co
ll its jo
to buy, a
ds may
y've
ent p
NOT

left to rig
Betsy Co
founder of t
Toronto gag
Philippa Jecchi
part-time Toronto RG who founded a gaggle
Athens, Greece, and Phyllis Creighton, who's bee
member since the Toronto gaggle was formed, perfo
at an Appeal for Peace, a citizens' conferen
at The Hague in the Netherlan

MONTREAL, QC

November 2001

The Montreal Raging
Grannies at peace march

Helen Hanna,
Lanie Melamed and
Joan Hadrill of the
Montreal Raging
Grannies at
International
Women's
Day 2001

PEACE ON EARTH

Left to ri...
Nancy Meinertzhagen, Marion Pa...
Nancy Roberts, Eva Munro, Barb...
Dacey and Elinor Egar Reyno...

WE'RE MAD AS HELL

Free Canada
NOT
FREE TRADE

am a ragin granny

...RLEY WARE
Daily News

...rannies rage
...ainst nuclear
...omarine plan

rection.

"It's hard to fight the military," Brightwell said – her hus-
...nt his entire career in
...es – "but we
...of our dol-

"Nuclear powered su...
rines are potential Ch...
a tin can," says ...
and Raging ...
Brightwell.

Raging ...
grandmo...
BC, w...
again...
ons w...
tum...

...d be
...u-

nu...
pu...
C...

i...
v...
a...

ri...
sai...
play...
gam...
und...

CONVERT THE N-SUBS

ROCHESTER, NY

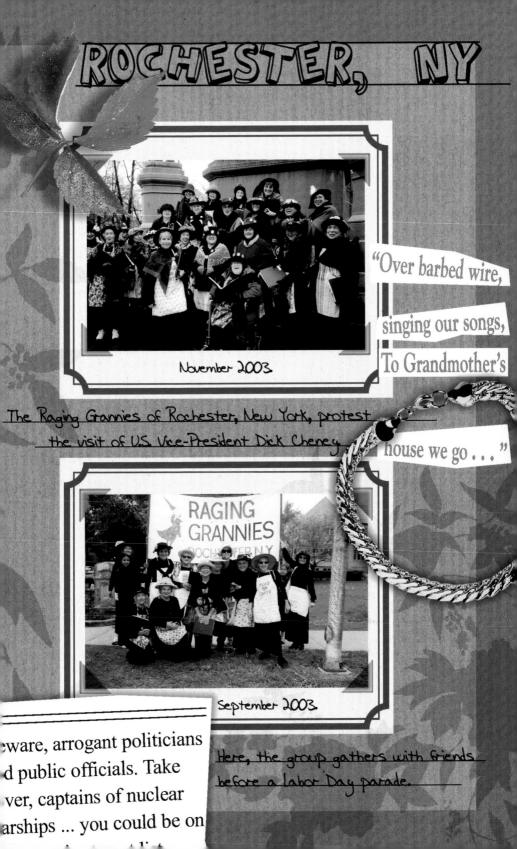

November 2003

"Over barbed wire, singing our songs, To Grandmother's house we go . . ."

The Raging Grannies of Rochester, New York, protest the visit of U.S. Vice-President Dick Cheney.

September 2003

eware, arrogant politicians
d public officials. Take
ver, captains of nuclear
arships ... you could be on

Here, the group gathers with friends before a Labor Day parade.

BUFFALO, NY

January 2004

This gaggle, which formed in November 2003, is pictured here at a rally against police brutality, racism and social injustice at the Buff. Science Museum.

November 2003

Raging against the FTAA (Free Trade Area of the Americas)

WESTERN MASSACHUSETTS

The Pioneer Valley Raging Grannies of Western Massachusetts sang to folks as they gathered for the workshop War and the Economy: Too Many Guns, Not Enough Butter in Amherst, Massachusetts.

the RAGING GRANNIES say no to war

EAST BAY, CA

The Raging Grannies of East Bay sing in a busy shopping centre in Berkeley, California, to urge voter registration and protest the elimination of rental financial aid.

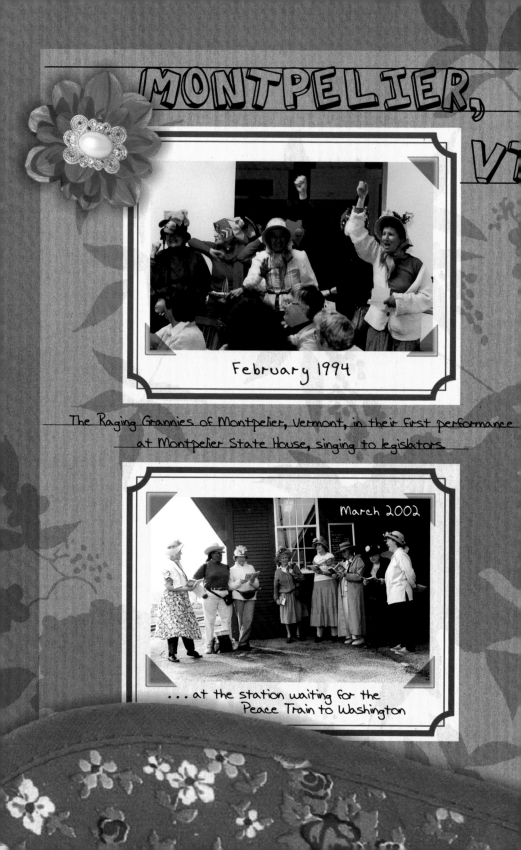

MONTPELIER, VT

February 1994

The Raging Grannies of Montpelier, Vermont, in their first performance at Montpelier State House, singing to legislators.

March 2002

...at the station waiting for the Peace Train to Washington

SEATTLE, WA

The Seattle Raging Grannies at the King County Administration Building, protesting the closure of a shelter for men.

The Seattle Raging Grannies pose for a photographer from Le Monde during the WTO talks.

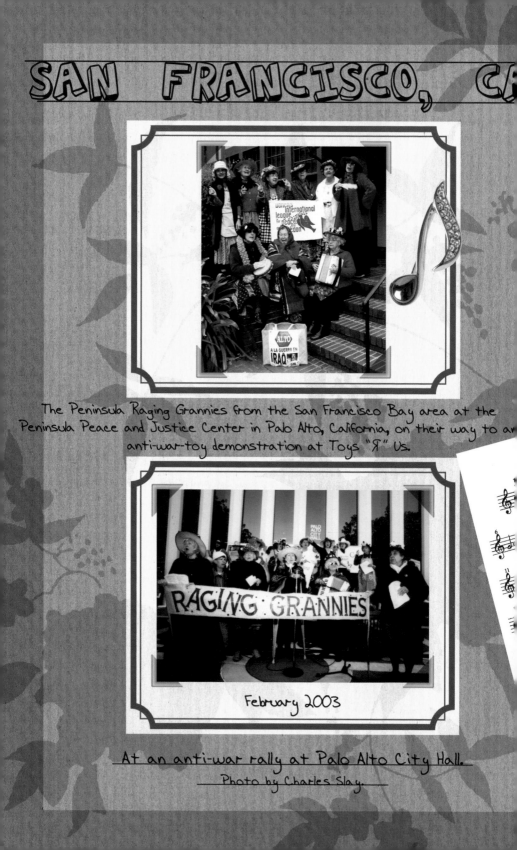

The Peninsula Raging Grannies from the San Francisco Bay area at the Peninsula Peace and Justice Center in Palo Alto, California, on their way to an anti-war-toy demonstration at Toys "Я" Us.

February 2003

At an anti-war rally at Palo Alto City Hall.
Photo by Charles Slay.

WINDSOR, ON/ DETROIT, MI

Left to right:
Bev Bloedel,
Motoko Huthwaite,
Kathy Russell,
Dolores Killewald,
Patricia Lay-Dorsey,
Emilia Grombala,
Judy Drylie
and Charlotte Kish

...at the 2nd Harvest for the Homeless, a fundraiser for Solid Ground Inc.

GRANNIES WITHOUT BORDERS

Left to right: Kathy Russell, Virginia "Birdie" Haynes, Emilia Grombala, Patricia Lay-Dorsey, Rosalia Haduch, Kim Redigan and Charlotte Kish their finery, pig snouts are provided, and everybody is invited to snort appropriate sound effects to cheer on the very best, or worst, nominee, whether bank chairman or sweatshop imperialist. After presenters read out their "accomplishments," the winners, such as Monsanto or Shell Oil, or at least their "deputies," come on stage to receive golden piggy banks, to vociferous piggy grunts and squeals. Local musicians — even the Grannies — provide musical interludes and there is always a special appearance by preschoolers, sometimes dressed up as three, or even eight, little pigs battling the capitalist wolf.

One year, our oldest Granny, Anita, donned a golden wig, a skirt more Minnie Mouse than mini, and, with a $49.95 price tag around her neck, sashayed around the stage as Barbie while we sang our protest song against the sweatshops that make Barbie dolls. Another year, a diva who usually sings opera went full throttle to inform us that "the world is run by assholes" and an upright Victorian who looks startlingly like Vladimir Lenin lectured us on the evils of the capitalist system. It is all great fun and good education, so it is no surprise that Windsor, Ontario, and possibly other cities have taken up the Golden Piggy Awards.

With the change in B.C. from an NDP to a Liberal government in 2001, the poor in Victoria have indeed gotten poorer. We have distributed fresh fruit to social assistance claimants on "Welfare Wednesdays" and we've taken food to street people and their dogs, too. We've supplied food, soap, bedding and clothes to street kids who, for a brief shining moment, were allowed to camp out safely beside Christ Church Anglican Cathedral until alleged drug use prompted the church to evict them. But by the end of 2001 we were discovering how large the problem of poverty had become and how tough it would be to change things.

In late 2002, we decided to take a satirical approach to the hard-heartedness of the B.C. Liberal government and collect "Pennies for the Premier," since he insisted he didn't have enough money to fund social programs. Dressed as the poor in Charles Dickens' time and suitably grubby, we panhandled through the streets along with other social protest groups, making it clear that we would only accept pennies. We can't remember now what happened to the money for "poor" Gordon Campbell, but we know it went to those who needed it more than he did. Anyway, we got a great reception from passersby, including those who were well-heeled. Even people who had voted Liberal hadn't expected the new government to carry out such attacks on the most vulnerable in our society.

The more we investigated the causes of poverty worldwide, the more readily we had to admit we are part of the problem ourselves because of our overconsumption of the world's resources. Sure, we carpool and brown-bag, we buy most of our clothes at thrift stores and we're not great spenders, but we're part of a wasteful North American society. So when we heard of *Adbusters* magazine's campaign to celebrate Buy Nothing Day on the last Friday in November — which is the busiest shopping day in the U.S., falling as it does just after their Thanksgiving — we thought we'd better join in. It's the day we promise not to shop. Not that we expect everybody to stop buying, but they might want to learn how their shopping habits support a system that relies on sweatshops and encourages acquisitiveness.

So one year we gathered outside the Eaton Centre in downtown Victoria (now the Bay Centre) with Ria dressed as a nurse brandishing a very large hypodermic needle to inoculate shoppers against "affluenza." Students from the University of Victoria joined us to hand out leaflets, and we were surprised by the guilt of a few shoppers, who rationalized that they were not really buying, just looking.

Actions with young people always give us a kick. We've been enchanted by recent competition from the Radical Cheerleaders, a University of Victoria contingent with pompoms, tattered stockings, short skirts and delightfully rude songs. Some Grannies wanted to try the same techniques, but then remembered how horribly we had failed at gumboot dancing in the style of South African miners. Instructed by an expert just back from Cape Town, we stomped and stamped in our best gardening boots, rehearsing for weeks for our appearance at a Granny Unconvention on Bowen Island, B.C. The applause was lukewarm. Now we are seriously considering belly dancing. It is supposed to be great for the waistline.

Many of us joined the Council of Canadians to protest the amazing profits made by banks that get rich by cutting staff and services. We'd sung at one bank because they dropped sponsorship of our environmental hero, David Suzuki. Now we decided to take on as many as we could. It was a pleasant surprise. We'd march into one of the downtown Victoria branches and start to sing and the waiting customers would break into smiles and even applause. It would be several minutes before the tellers could roust out whoever handled security and have us evicted. We would leave ever so slowly, and then head to the bank across the street, to sing for another group of unhappy customers. Most of us switched long ago to local credit unions.

Our Santa Claus forays have not been so readily appreciated. Right from the beginning we decided to campaign against war toys and war games because we are convinced they encourage violence. At first, store owners showed the true spirit of the season. Toy City even brought us mugs of hot chocolate when we warbled outside their store in 1987, but the uniformed security officer at the local Tillicum Mall (*tillicum* means "friend" in Chinook) summoned us to the manager's office, where we got a severe reprimand for distracting his patrons from shopping till they dropped.

We knew what to do about that the next Christmas — call the press for Round Two. This time the manager left his office, threatened to call the cops and found himself on TV, getting red in the face at a gaggle of Grannies in scarlet coats, red stockings and green hats who insisted on carolling at him about GI Joe. Two young boys witnessing the engagement said we had a good point and our clothes were awesome.

We've tried again, meeting a similarly frosty reception from other mall managers in Victoria. We've brought along Mrs. Claus, a.k.a. Marya Nyland. We've dressed ourselves up as overstuffed elves and rearranged the stock so that war toys got shelved on the bottom and out of sight. We're sure of the rightness of our cause, but we also recognize it's tough enough for harassed parents to go Christmas shopping without getting advice from a bunch of Grannies. Yet the campaign against war toys continues to involve Grannies right across Canada. Not one group has yet been arrested for "trespassing" in a shopping mall, but they have all had great encounters with management, the press and sometimes the police.

At Christmas 2002, we tried it again inside Toys "Я" Us in the Mayfair Mall, Victoria's biggest shopping precinct. The very young security lad kept trying to invite us into the manager's office. We know better than to fall for that one; we insist on staying public. So the manager emerged and threatened to call the cops if we didn't shut up. We told him to go ahead, and we warbled through the halls, singing until our throats went dry and our feet gave out, and still no police came. When the manager reappeared an hour later, without a single policeman, we were so exhausted that we agreed to cut a deal and leave the mall, but to go out singing. The campaign continues. In 2003 we donned bright orange T-shirts that read "War Toys, War Games, Don't Buy Them" back and front and paraded through the malls, singing, receiving a thumbs-up from shoppers and only frazzled disapproval from security staff.

Thinking it might be easier and safer to reach our audience at Victoria's annual Santa Claus Parade, we have infiltrated it on several occasions, knowing it would be useless to apply legitimately. We simply spliced ourselves into the parade, between fake reindeer and jolly elves, with a megaphone and leaflets advising parents where to buy peaceful toys. (We do try to be positive where we can.) We've got a lot of applause, but maybe that's because of our hats.

It's hard to strike a balance. If nobody likes us, nobody is going to listen to our message. But if we let ourselves be turned into lovable local characters, we're doomed. However, we felt quite flattered when Peter Grant, a local author, devoted a whole page to us in his 1994 guidebook *Victoria from Sidney to Sooke*, alongside photographs of the ubiquitous flower baskets and orcas, or killer whales.[1] He believed in our anti-war message.

Chatelaine magazine interviewed us in 1991 for an article entitled "How to start a citizen's action group." They photographed us lying down in a circle and looking very strange indeed.[2]

Granny press interviews often show up the differences among us. Sid Tafler, a well-known Victoria writer, trapped us at a Granny meeting for an article in *Fifty Plus*, the magazine of the Canadian Association of Retired Persons. Betty was in a sour mood after a battle of wills with a new computer program and declared: "There is no hope. The powers that be are far greater than ever before."[3] Ria announced that we were like snowflakes: a few billion of us could stop a train. Freda claimed we had defeated the Multilateral Agreement on Investment, so there. Alison said we were the leavening in the bread, and Anita said she'd like to be the blade of grass that splits the concrete. This was much more fun than the usual article about our hats.

Canadian journalist and historian Peter Newman, in one of his *Maclean's* magazine columns, once advised an embattled corporation to hire "Victoria's Raging Grannies to sit around your boardroom table. They'll rant all day and they never quit."[4]

British mystery writer Dorothy Sayers understood: "Time and trouble will tame an advanced young woman but an advanced old woman is uncontrollable by any earthly force."[5] We were certainly advancing.

Ralph Nader, the American consumer advocate, said that Grannies had found a way "to break through without ever losing their dignity,"[6] but then he'd never seen us at one of our more outrageous gigs or protests.

Warren Magnusson, a sociology professor at the University of Victoria, put us into his book *Canadian Politics*, but most of us would barely recognize ourselves as "warm, gentle, humorous, unthreatening, eminently respectable people who speak in tones of grandmotherly reproach: 'Why are you doing these things, my children?'"[7]

Carole Roy, a friend of some of the early Grannies, wrote her M. A. thesis on us and gave a lecture at UVic, where she declared that she had found our common thread — most of us had experienced sexism and ageism, had a sense of being under threat and a strong sense of our own personal history. She said our most powerful weapon was our smile and our ability to shatter the stereotype of the older, quieter and understated middle-class woman. She has gone on to dissect us for her Ph.D. at the Ontario Institute for Studies in Education, grandly titled "Meddlesome Crones with Outrageous Hats, Humorous Songs, and Daring Dissent: The Raging Grannies' Creative and Educational Protests."

British Columbia Woman to Woman found a political scientist to analyze us. Dr. Somer Brodribb, from UVic, said many women use irony, ridicule and humour. "In Africa, women will encircle a chief who has displeased them. Then they'll sing him down. They make their displeasure known through ridicule and shaming."[8] Might that work with Premier Gordon Campbell? But what about his phalanx of security guards?

Britain's *Saga Magazine* for wrinklies ran a colour spread about us in 2001. Author Simon Birch wondered why such respectable senior citizens were "so hot under their frilly collars" but admired our refusal to grow old gracefully.[9] The article resulted in many e-mails from British women eager to start their own Granny gaggles.

We rationalize all this media exposure not as a grab at fame, but as a way to spread our message, and we do try to be modest. But if famed American folkie Pete Seeger calls us "unstoppable" and celebrated Canadian singers seek us out — Bruce Cockburn wanted his photograph taken with us, and Valdy called us in as his backup singers for a Victoria Earth Walk gig — it's hard to be humble.

However, we do feel like David facing Goliath in taking on the issue of free trade with the United States. We don't like it. Right from our beginnings we saw it as an attack on Canadian sovereignty. That threat had incited our first venture into a national Raging Granny campaign when, at an early Unconvention held at Crescent Beach outside Vancouver, we copied the newly formed Halifax gaggle by pouring tea into the Pacific Ocean in a campaign from "sea to sea." We solemnly trotted down to the beach with assorted teapots and sprinkled the waves. We considered it an echo of the Boston Tea Party when the rebels chose to dump imported British tea as a symbol of their desire for independence from the colonial yoke. In turn, we didn't want the U.S. telling us what to drink, what to eat or how to spend our money. With the Council of Canadians, we protested attacks on our way of life threatened by the adoption of the free-trade agreement with the U.S.

Later, we began to see that the North American Free Trade Agreement (NAFTA) was more than a sovereignty issue for Canada. We were heading into the war against global capitalism and we were learning a new word — globalization. Labour unions, environmentalists and non-governmental organizations woke up and rose up in anger against the power of corporations, which were the real movers behind free trade. We weren't just being taken over by our neighbours to the south; we were becoming victims of globalization with deregulated markets, unrestrained foreign investment and unrestricted trade. Prime Minister Mulroney had declared in 1984 that Canada was "open for business," and Simon Reisman, a retired trade bureaucrat, was being paid $1,000 a day to run the Trade Negotiations Office in Ottawa, which we felt was not standing up for Canada.

We naively thought things would be different when Jean Chrétien became prime minister in October 1993, because he had spent nine years fighting Mulroney's free-trade policies. Boy, were we wrong. We felt our health care, culture and education were all being threatened. Even Canada Post was subject to complaints of unfair competition by multinational courier companies. Next, Canadian companies were forced to add neurotoxic MMT (methylcyclopentadienyl manganese tricarbonyl) to the gas in our cars, though it had previously been banned as a health threat. Finally, in 2002, B.C. would be faced by oppressive duties on softwood lumber exports to the U.S. Logging towns became ghost towns as unemployment spread.

More of us joined the Council of Canadians, wrote letters to Ottawa and felt more and more helpless. Free trade spread to Latin

America and moved into Asia, with sweatshops doing the work once done in North America and paying workers in pennies. Soon the top global corporations were richer than many nations and we were learning an alphabet soup of acronyms for the alliances of governments and corporations. One of the most powerful of these was the Asia-Pacific Economic Cooperation Alliance; its slogan was "APEC Means Business."

Indonesian dictator Suharto cracked down hard on any opposition when he hosted the 1994 APEC meeting. The Philippine government blacklisted at least 100 overseas activists going to the 1996 meeting in that country, and refused them entry. Then the government bulldozed the shanties of 33,000 families to improve the landscape around the conference site and to open up "APEC friendship lanes" for limousines. (Betty, always the devil's advocate, told us she saw those shanties during her two-year stay in the Far East and thought then they should be flattened, but was wise enough to add that the residents should have been offered alternate housing.) In 1997 it was Canada's turn to host the APEC meeting, and it was held in Vancouver.

Inger went to the People's Summit, organized in downtown Vancouver by the non-governmental organizations just before delegates arrived on November 24. Then she opted for the barricades, which were being set up outside the University of British Columbia's Museum of Anthropology, chosen as a retreat where the APEC leaders would, supposedly, be safe from protesters.

Inger reported, "I went with a young friend, Sarah, because I was worried she might get hurt and thought maybe I could protect her. I never really imagined there would be pepper spray. I was behind her, so I didn't get sprayed in the face, but she did and it really hurt. We didn't know what to do so we tried bathing her eyes in hot water and that only made it worse. There were hundreds of kids there behind the barricade, half a mile from the APEC meeting, all of them peaceful and all of them with a legal right to be there. Then along came Sergeant Pepper [RCMP Staff Sergeant Hughie Stewart], aiming his gun full of pepper spray." Prime

Minister Chrétien joked later that he put pepper on his plate and refused to appear before the public inquiry that ensued.

Later, we learned that Jaggi Singh, an anti-APEC organizer, had been arrested the day before the meeting on a charge of assaulting a security guard by speaking loudly into a megaphone too close to the man's ear two weeks earlier. Then Craig Jones, a lifelong Liberal supporter, was arrested for hanging three small signs calling for "Free Speech," "Democracy" and "Human Rights" on a coat rack behind the security fence.

When the inquiry's report finally appeared in 2001, the finger of blame for the overreaction was pointed at the Prime Minister's Office, where saving the Indonesian dictator from even the most polite protest had been seen as more important than free speech. When Chrétien attended a 1998 fundraiser at a Vancouver hotel, the cops again clamped down hard on protesters, giving rise to what became known as the Riot at the Hyatt.

One of the documents that surfaced at the APEC inquiry, a military document marked "secret" and "for Canadian eyes only," was an RCMP list of "anti-Canadian forces" that constituted a potential threat to APEC leaders. There were the Raging Grannies, alongside Amnesty International and the Anglican Church. Embarrassingly, we were listed as only "a minor threat." We'd have to change that.

Thank goodness we again had some new recruits to help us. When Anne Moon moved to Victoria in 1995, she hoped to join the Grannies, whose fame had spread to her Toronto home, but a friend told her there was a long waiting list — actually, that was a tactic to discourage women who weren't utterly committed — so she didn't pursue us. She had been a member of every major political party, seeking to support the candidate rather than his or her policies. But, bruised by the Tory rout of the NDP in Ontario, she became one of many "Mike Harris refugees," retiring to the west coast and anxious to volunteer wherever she was needed.

One day she and her daughter were wandering along the causeway in Victoria's Inner Harbour when they spied a bunch of bizarrely clad women busily dusting the statue of Captain James Cook and warning tourists about the dangers posed by a visiting U.S. nuclear warship berthed in Esquimalt: It might be out of sight, but it was still capable of releasing radioactive dust or even blowing up Victoria. Raging Grannies in action.

"My daughter dragged me over to them and announced, 'You want my mother. She can write and she can sing,'" Anne later recalled. "Those Grannies could resist the RCMP, but they couldn't stand up to my daughter." Anne has taken singing lessons and had a career as a journalist and public-relations officer for causes she believes in. Born in England, growing up as "a bossy big sister" and surviving boarding school, she's tough and she's a great organizer. She keeps track of the Grannies when we're out en masse. She organizes our getaways. "We don't call them retreats. The Grannies never retreat; they advance." Anne echoes her role model, Nellie

Mary, Kathy, Doran, Betty and Inger spread our anti-nuclear message in the busy tourist corridor across from the Empress Hotel. (JOHN McKAY/VICTORIA *TIMES COLONIST* PHOTO)

McClung, the Canadian feminist made famous for saying "Never retreat, never explain, never apologize, get the thing done and let them howl."[10] A great Granny motto.

We knew she was one of us when she reported that she had dyed her white hair purple with grape Kool-Aid in a fruitless attempt to liven up a seniors' bus trip. It wasn't long before she made her mark. The Victoria City Council announced an open house to proudly display plans for a revived downtown, or how to make developers even richer. Grannies turned up with Anne in the lead, blasting on a newly acquired whistle. "We're here to blow the whistle on greedy developers," she shrieked.

Laura Fisher came to us courtesy of the Edmonton Raging Grannies. She grew up in the U.S., the daughter of a career army officer and a southern belle, and married Tony, her high-school sweetheart, after just one year of college. He went off to war in Korea and she took care of the three kids, who, in the early 1960s, marched beside their parents on the streets of Santa Barbara, California, singing "We Shall Overcome" in support of Martin Luther King Jr. When the family moved to Edmonton, Tony taught anthropology and Laura joined the Voice of Women, sheltered American draft dodgers and helped found the Edmonton Committee to End the War in Vietnam. When feminism caught up with her, she got her degree in education and worked as a home economics teacher.

With retirement in 1992 she discovered the Edmonton Raging Grannies, who outfitted her with a Gibson girl pink hat and lacy shawl that she still wears today. In 1998 the Fishers moved to Cobble Hill on Vancouver Island, where Laura promptly presented herself as a displaced Granny to the Cowichan Valley gaggle. The Cowichan Grannies were more interested in local issues, so Laura turned to the Victoria gaggle, which was open — perhaps too open — to wider issues. She became a member of both gaggles, but later found her heart was closer to her Victoria sisters and that we had enough work to keep her busy.

We needed all hands on deck because there was new urgency to our primary mission: getting defence and civil authorities to take seriously the threat of nuclear accidents. Our confidence in the military, its marksmanship and its preparedness for disaster is not very high. Indeed, Victorians were severely shaken in 1996 when Pete's Tent & Awning in Esquimalt was hit by a dummy missile fired from HMCS *Regina*. Friendly fire indeed!

In May 1997 the Nuclear Safety and Control Act was revised. Grannies were initially pleased because it addressed safety of persons and the environment. But a closer look revealed that the act does not apply to "a nuclear-powered or nuclear-capable naval vessel of a foreign state that is invited into Canada by Her Majesty in right of Canada." That exception, however, did not mean that Raging Grannies intended to cease protesting. Canada is still a nuclear-weapons-free state, being a signatory of the Non-Proliferation Treaty. So, it was full steam ahead and keep on nagging about every nuclear warship that came to B.C.

We had to do more homework. We learned that most nuclear-powered vessels were submarines, but there were also aircraft carriers, cruisers and icebreakers. The United States, United Kingdom, France, China and some of the former Soviet republics build and operate nuclear-powered vessels. Worldwide, there are about 400 nuclear reactors at sea or in port. Currently only American or British nuclear-capable naval vessels are allowed in Canadian waters, and only at three sites: Halifax, Esquimalt and Nanoose Bay, near Nanaimo. Canada receives about 25 visits a year from American warships capable of carrying nuclear weapons.

While the U.S. and Britain won't disclose their nuclear assets, neither country routinely deploys tactical nuclear weapons, but you never know, because they will "neither confirm nor deny." In other words, they won't tell us. These naval vessels often make routine goodwill visits to foreign ports, including those three places in Canada, mainly for crew rest and relaxation, but also as a means of promoting harmony and understanding, which may benefit coordination of activities in times of need. The visits certainly benefit the pockets of local pubs and madams.

We remember when Prime Minister Pierre Trudeau announced that "Canada is the first country in the world with nuclear capabilities that chose not to use them for military purposes."[11] The Grannies and the entire Canadian peace movement believe that it is hypocritical of the Canadian government to allow vessels capable of bearing nuclear arms into Canada when we are a nuclear-weapons-free country. They come here because of our treaties with NATO and NORAD, and although the Americans tell us there are no nuclear weapons on any ships coming into our ports, we doubt this is true for the Los Angeles class submarines or the huge Trident I and II submarines that slither past our shores.

Betty, who was appointed to the Esquimalt Emergency Preparedness Committee after asking a pointed question at an

An armada of Grannies (left to right, Mary, Inger, unidentified supporter, Betty, Alison) launches from the Esquimalt Nation reserve, preparing to kayak to the Department of National Defence dockyard to protest a nuclear-capable submarine. (JOHN McKAY/VICTORIA *TIMES COLONIST* PHOTO)

all-candidates meeting, started asking even more questions. We did get a few changes made. When we insisted that it wasn't good enough to send water surrounding the nuclear subs to Vancouver for radiation tests, CFB Esquimalt began to test it on-site and installed monitors to detect airborne radiation. Esquimalt City Council told Betty not to worry because Ottawa and Washington had everything in hand. With no emergency plans for civilians, DND seems to believe radiation would stop at the gates of the base.

Betty did suggest several times that a leaflet outlining what to do in any nuclear emergency (remembering the fallout from Chernobyl) should be available for all concerned citizens. She even procured the pamphlet that Ontario Hydro was forced to release to residents in Pickering, Ontario, after problems with the nuclear power system there. But Esquimalt Council and DND were not interested. "Don't worry, dear," was the response.

We were also worried about the possibility of nuclear accidents in Nanoose Bay, so we joined the Nanoose Conversion Campaign (NCC), whose members were trying to return the whole area around the testing site to its original tranquility and, maybe, find employment for security guards as nature guides. The NCC had been protesting for years, but now their researchers had found out something quite startling: The seabed in Nanoose Bay did not belong to the federal government; it belonged to B.C. and was licensed to the feds. And since 300 to 400 torpedoes were being tested in a year, leaving trails of copper wire and other debris on the seabed to pollute the Strait of Georgia, we thought B.C.'s Minister of Environment, Paul Ramsey, ought to be interested, especially as the NDP provincial government had several issues it wanted to raise with Ottawa. The NCC members wanted an appointment with him; maybe we could help.

In October 1996, Fran wrote a letter to the minister, requesting a meeting. It closed with: "If we do not get a reply to this request before November 13, we shall be stopping by your office."

Grannies pose at the Esquimalt Nation reserve prior to delivering flowers to a nuclear-capable submarine. Back (left to right): Alison, Fran. Front: Ria, Betty, Anita.

Silence. So three weeks later, on November 14, Betty, Alison, Freda, Fran, Anita, Jean McLaren and Grace Tickson walked past indignant security guards, climbed over velvet rope barriers and trooped up the stairs to the office of the minister of environment, where we eventually met Ramsey's ministerial assistant, Bryan

McIvor. He insisted he had no knowledge of our letter or the letters from the Nanoose Conversion Campaign, had never heard of the seabed licence and failed to understand its significance to British Columbia. He told us firmly he could do nothing for us: Ramsey was out of town, the person who makes his appointments was out of town, we really should leave and try again, with more letters, to set up an appointment.

We watched his face blanch as Betty plumped herself into a comfortable leather chair and said not to worry, her car was in a long-term parking spot and she had all day. Fran brought out her usual vegan sandwich to munch. Alison had her knitting. Jean found another comfortable chair, and the others also showed no sign of leaving the congested office. A secretary politely offered chairs to Freda and Grace. After some time and some behind-the-scenes conferring by telephone, McIvor promised he would call Betty the next day with a firm appointment that would take place within two weeks. We all shook hands on the deal and left.

Two weeks later, we trimmed down our numbers to be more effective. Betty and Fran represented the Raging Grannies. Ivan Bulic, Norm Abbey and a Sierra Defence Fund lawyer, Jane Luke, spoke for the Nanoose Conversion Campaign. We planned to meet at the Embassy Restaurant, right across from the Legislative Buildings, at 9 A.M. to plot our strategy. But word had spread and we were inundated by high-powered help who also had a message for Ramsey: a peace activist from Sechelt, Denise Lagasse, with her four-year-old daughter, Miska; Joan Russow, soon to become the Green Party's leader; Fred Knelman, a long-time anti-nuclear guru from the University of Victoria; and still more activists. The security guards unhooked the velvet rope, but only for seven of us.

Ramsey was cordial, forthright and interested. He was flanked by three lawyers. Ivan, Norm and Jane did the talking; Betty and Fran took notes, adding a few questions. The half-hour appointment stretched to an hour. Ramsey seemed attentive and concerned about U.S. torpedo testing and about environmental degradation caused by military activity in the Strait of Georgia, but he held out little hope that anything could change.

To our surprise, some months later it looked as if somebody had been listening to us. Premier Glen Clark threatened to close down the test range, refusing to renew the federal government's seabed licence. He was using the provincial ownership of the coastal seabed in an effort to force the federal government to stop American commercial fishboats from catching salmon hatched in Canada. In 1999, the feds responded by expropriating the seabed.

The Grannies didn't like it. We decided it was time for tit-for-tat. We would expropriate a federally owned island (well, it was an island at high tide) off the coast of B.C. We picked out the territory to conquer and consulted maps to make certain our rock off Macaulay Point in Esquimalt was included in Ottawa's jurisdiction — in this case, the Canadian Forces Base Esquimalt.

This is Pacifica, the federally owned island (it was an island only at high tide) we named and liberated from the Department of National Defence after the latter expropriated Nanoose Bay so it could continue weapons testing there.

We issued an invitation to the local press, gathered our forces and, on September 9, 1999, a very windy day, we sallied forth in gumboots, not at dawn's early light but after an excellent picnic lunch. Alison, carrying the Raging Granny flag made by Ria, with two deck chairs tucked under her other arm, and Fran as backup squad, carrying several more deck chairs, scurried along the narrow path on the Macaulay Point cliffs. The wind caught the large flag, almost turning Alison into Mary Poppins soaring off over the Strait of Juan de Fuca. An agile *Times Colonist* photographer ran ahead to capture the very moment when the conquering heroines triumphed over the rocks and the tide and made it to "our" island. The reporter from the *Esquimalt News* was not as enthusiastic. She was cold, took a few notes and left.

The rest of the invasion force, including auxiliary Granny Jane Brett, advanced more cautiously than our gallant leaders. We slid on our bums down the cliff, gingerly crossed the sharp rocks and clambered onto our rocky domain unopposed. There we sang our new national anthem, "Pacifica, Pacifica, Our Own Pacific Island," and pitched a tent to establish our intention to stay.

Janet Hawksley, another auxiliary Granny, and Anita stayed ashore, sitting on a park bench and issuing visa/immigration certificates to the few residents walking by. The locals, of course, are of the considered opinion that Raging Grannies are demented. Most rolled their eyes heavenward and threw up their hands in disbelief. Perhaps one or two had some understanding of why we were doing what we were doing. We only had two visitors to our newly conquered island. One was a man in a suit, who hailed us from shore, wanting to assure himself that we were unarmed. Perhaps he thought we might be preparing to free the illegal Chinese immigrants then being held nearby in a closed compound. If he was a federal agent, and he probably was, he didn't seem to care that we had conquered part of Canada. In truth, Immigration Minister Elinor Caplan was that very day visiting the incarcerated "boat people" and we had invited her to become the first foreign diplomat we would receive. We think the federal agent warned her off.

The other visitor arrived by canoe, bringing food from Green Cuisine, a local vegetarian restaurant frequented by Fran. He didn't stay long. The wind had increased, the waves were becoming dangerous, and he wanted to get the heck out of there, fast. We cheered him on his way to calmer waters, ate the snacks and hunkered down against the wind, convincing ourselves that the Canadian frigate sailing around out there in the Strait of Juan de Fuca was observing us through powerful telescopes and probably getting ready either to bombard us or to dispatch a landing barge to arrest us all. Eventually the tide came in. Not wanting to get wet, we waded ashore and went home.

Alison (left) and Fran take possession of Pacifica with lawn chairs and the Granny flag. (BRUCE STOTESBURY/VICTORIA *TIMES COLONIST* PHOTO)

Next day's *Times Colonist* had a dramatic colour picture of our invasion. Like the Spaniards, who first arrived on these shores in the 1700s, we should have erected a cross and buried a bottle proclaiming our new possession. But we had no empty bottle, not even a beer bottle, and our rocky island was undiggable.

That December, Alison and Betty had a chat with the base commander at a Christmas party. "Yes," he said, "we knew you were there." From the tone of his voice, it seemed he couldn't have cared less. Next time, we'll have to hammer in a bronze plaque to mark our claim. Better still, if Ottawa ever turns Nanoose Bay over to British Columbia again, and if B.C. stops those nuclear subs coming into its waters, we might give our island back. Until then, Pacifica is ours, but the squabble between the province and the feds over Nanoose continued.

We weren't the only ones angry about Ottawa expropriating the seabed at Nanoose Bay. The Society for the Promotion of Environmental Conservation (SPEC) went straight to the Supreme Court of B.C. In 2002 the court overturned the 1999 expropriation of Nanoose, agreeing that there had been a breach in the procedure because the report by the expropriation-hearing officer did not fairly represent the level of opposition expressed by thousands of British Columbians. One year later, on May 30, 2003, the federal Court of Appeal reversed the Supreme Court decision. So the feds still control the seabed at Nanoose Bay.

We will reoccupy Pacifica if Ottawa becomes particularly nasty, though the provincial Liberal government that took power in 2001 seems to have no quarrel with the feds. We still have our red Granny banner.

Sung to the tune of "School Days,"
by Gus Edwards and Will D. Cobb, 1907; lyrics by Jane Mackey

War toys, war toys,
Good old-fashioned war toys,
From pop guns, tin soldiers and wooden swords
To Rambo, machine guns and Skeletor.
These are the things for which kids yearn.
Think of the useful stuff they learn,
Like how to inflict a laser burn
On all of their buddies at school.
[Kazoo first four lines]
If they can't have what's on TV
They're screwed up psychologically.
They must be prepared for World War Three
While they're still impressionable kids.

FOREIGN AFFAIRS

As a woman I have no country.
As a woman my country is the whole world.
— *Virginia Woolf*

I n March 1999, war broke out in the Balkans. It was a highly complex war that we found difficult to understand, but we had to protest. We continue to believe that war represents failure and resolves nothing. Canada's foreign minister, Lloyd Axworthy, spoke about preferring a diplomatic approach to military action, but the stories of atrocities in Kosovo and entreaties from other NATO countries were drawing Canada into the fight. We sent in our CF-18 bombers and deployed support personnel on the ground. Indeed, we have had troops in the area ever since the fighting began, trying to restore peace.

Grannies tried to believe Vaclav Havel, president of the Czech Republic, when he explained: "It is neither an easy struggle nor a popular one, and there can be different opinions on its strategy and tactics, but no person of sound judgment can deny one thing. This is probably the first war ever fought that is not being fought in the name of interests but in the name of certain principles and values.

If it is possible to say about a war that it is ethical or that it is fought for ethical reasons, it is true of this war."[1]

But war is war, and Victoria's peace movement reacted. On March 27, 1999, a Granny group protested the war at the B.C. legislature. We were not alone in being horrified by a militant NATO and our own country's participation. CNN-TV told us that protests drew thousands of demonstrators throughout Europe and the United States as NATO missiles pounded Yugoslavia.

Starting on April 3, a small contingent of peace people, including the Raging Grannies, held a vigil every Saturday morning at the cenotaph in front of the B.C. legislature. To avoid conflict with a local, vocal group of Serbians, we arranged for them to hold their vigil at 11 A.M. and the local anti-war group (with no Balkan affiliations) had their vigil at noon, after the Serbians had laid a red rose on the cenotaph and gone home. This arrangement continued through the brief, intense war in Yugoslavia, although the groups involved became smaller. The war in Kosovo was the lead story for all TV news broadcasts. We were assailed with heart-wrenching pictures of refugees as more than 130,000 ethnic Albanians sought shelter outside the Serb province in the first week of the war. But we were also inundated with press briefings by NATO generals seeming to glorify war, and graphic film coverage on TV detailing the effects of precision bombing.

Bomb them and then aid them. We didn't buy it. The Balkan war was very difficult to comprehend, given the long history of religious and ethnic conflict in the region. As Grannies, all we could do was light candles and write to our foreign minister, condemning the bombing of Serbia and Canada's apparent willingness to let NATO become the military arm of the United Nations.

The war was such a muddle that even after it had ended, nobody could agree on the number of civilian casualties. NATO claimed only 500. Yugoslavia claimed 5,000. The Western world seemed more interested in how much the war had cost. According to a 1999 study by the BBC and *Jane's Defence Weekly*, costs of the 78-day bombing were over $5 billion Canadian, and estimated costs for rebuilding Yugoslavia would be seven times that. However, not much rebuilding by Western powers went on. The former Yugoslavia soon replaced Albania as Europe's poorest nation and world attention shifted to The Hague for the trial of Slobodan Milosevic for war crimes.

The Balkan war seemed very far from Canada and far too complex. We thought we knew a little more about trade wars that directly affected us, so when we discovered that the World Trade Organization was to meet in Seattle in November 1999, we decided to join a protest. We knew what the WTO was all about — big business dictating to the world.

Freda and Inger went early, to the teach-in organized by non-governmental organizations from around the world. Fran, Anne, Laura and Alison joined them at the downtown Green Tortoise hostel ($8 a night, with breakfast, six to a room with bunk beds and a sink), ready for the rally next day, organized by the labour unions. We were impressed by the pre-rally gathering for seniors, complete with sticky buns and free rain capes and an escort to choice seats in the Seattle Center stadium, where we listened to speeches and then joined the authorized protest march. The Seattle Grannies had invited us to sing and march with them and the hundred thousand other protesters with disparate banners but a common cause. We headed toward the WTO meeting in the Convention Center, getting close but not too close to the action. We held hands to stay together. There were turtles ("please save them," said a banner) and Teamsters, Zapatistas and nurses, church folk and anarchists. Thousands of other protesters had already blocked access to the WTO's first day of meetings. When union organizers tried to lead us back to the buses instead of letting us join the sit-down in the streets, we had to think fast. The Seattle Grannies had laid on supper at a Granny supporter's house on Capitol Hill. They pleaded with us to go with them, and we were their guests, so reluctantly we went.

As we headed back to the hostel that night, the air was thick with tear gas and there were helicopters buzzing overhead.

Victoria Granny Anne Moon, left, joins the Seattle Raging Grannies at the Battle in Seattle, protesting against the World Trade Organization in November 1999.

Somebody had smashed windows at McDonald's and vandalized a few banks, but we saw police watching the vandals and doing nothing to stop them. Garbage cans were burning at street corners and the sidewalks were littered with shattered glass. The cops ignored the chaos. We asked one of them what was going on but he refused to reply, so we retreated to the hostel. Later, the City estimated damage of $3 million with $10 million in lost business.

"You naughty Grannies. You're grounded," the hostel night clerk told us when we sneaked back, two minutes after the curfew imposed by the Seattle police.

Next day, Alison went into the streets and came up against phalanxes of the National Guard, armoured carriers and mounted police face-to-face with protesters who were armed only with scarves against tear gas. President Bill Clinton had come to town and the police had orders to crack down on protests. Seattle looked like a war zone.

"I tried talking to the cops, hoping to keep them calm, but very soon I was alongside the protesters, yelling at National Guardsmen dressed up like Darth Vader, 'What would your mother say?'" Alison reported. "I had a shouting match with a policewoman who tried to push me off the road and [I] tried to comfort a young girl who was crying and terrified. Then a line of National Guardsmen ran at the kids sitting down and dragged some of them to a waiting bus. I rushed back to get Granny reinforcements."

At the hostel, we had to bang the windows shut as the armoured cars came down our street (which was far from the security zone), lobbing tear-gas shells though there were no protesters in sight. Fran and Anne were coughing badly, but we had promised to join a women's anti-WTO concert in Pike Place Market, so we went out. It was barely three blocks away, but we never got there. Everything was quiet and most of the market was shut down, but along came the tear-gas goons and soon we were running for shelter. The Seattle Grannies reported later that it was just as bad where many of them lived, on Capitol Hill, in a ritzier part of town. Security had chased people out of the city centre up the hill, thereby enraging citizens who had never thought they'd be targeted just like the protesters.

Five hundred people were arrested that day, including a blind man and his dog, and they were held for days while sympathizers chanted outside the jail. They weren't released until the WTO delegates had gone home. The police and National Guard had used plastic bullets, tear gas, pepper spray, truncheons and water cannons. The evidence was out there in all the media, showing National Guardsmen kicking protesters and dragging young people off the sidewalk and into buses heading for jail.

This was the equipment carried by the police: double-canister gas masks, semi-automatic guns loaded with plastic shot, plastic handcuffs, leg guards, slash-resistant gloves, face shields, riot batons, chemical grenades, pyrotechnic grenades, expulsion grenades, rubber bullet grenades, grenade launchers, aerosol tear-gas tanks, rubber bullet munitions, ballistic helmets, magazine pouches, Kevlar body armour, but no visible badges or ID. And the protesters? The mayor of Seattle declared it was illegal for civilians to wear gas masks.

The protests and the repression gave the WTO some very bad press. Reporters seemed surprised by the organization and effectiveness of the protest and alarmed by police tactics, which would be implemented more fully in Genoa, Italy, in 2001, at the next international trade conference. The Italian security forces were vicious. One protester was killed, others dragged from their beds and beaten. The world was horrified by photographs of men smashing their batons into helpless young people who seemed to have no part in any vandalism.

Some of us left Seattle with feelings of guilt, even though we thought our presence had spread the word that it wasn't just a few young hotheads who were fed up with globalization. The Grannies had made *Time, USA Today*, the *Wall Street Journal* and the *International Herald Tribune*, but we asked ourselves later if we had done all we could. Why didn't we stay and join protesters outside the jail? Could we have done more to cool the police bullies, to stop vandalism, to get our message across?

We promised to do better at a meeting of NATO set for Victoria in November 2001. Surely Victoria police wouldn't get violent. We in Victoria have lost our two-horse mounted police patrol to budget cuts but now have something much cheaper — a kennel of German shepherd dogs. They are kept in the background and have yet to be let loose on crowds.

We attended meetings to organize the protests against the NATO conference, especially those concerned with media coverage. The Battle in Seattle had proved the value of alternative media in spreading the word, and we wanted to be part of that process. We talked about ways to breach the 50-block security zone that the Victoria police were contemplating. Could we infiltrate by sea? What about balloons? Or kites? We wrote the police, offering our sage Granny advice. We invited other Granny groups to join us. And then Victoria City Council, worried about the estimated $4,700,000 cost of policing, withdrew the invitation to NATO and the Victoria meeting was cancelled. The next WTO meeting was in Qatar, on the Persian Gulf. No Grannies there, and no other protesters admitted to the country either.

Since then, other Granny groups have taken up the challenge. A number of Grannies from Ottawa, Toronto and Montreal went to Quebec City in April 2001 to protest a meeting of the Free Trade Area of the Americas, joining 60,000 other protesters. Just as in Seattle, hooligans broke store windows, threw petrol bombs and started fires. Some of them, we suspect, were disguised security officers, acting as *agents provocateurs*. Four hundred people were arrested, few of whom had taken any part in the violence. The majority of marchers were peaceful and stayed behind the notorious "wall of shame," a four-kilometre-long, three-metre-high chain-and-concrete fence erected to keep protesters away from the "suits." At the fence 6,000 police and security forces were massed to use water cannons, pepper spray and guns that shot hard-coated plastic bullets. Even the delegates attending the conference could smell the tear gas.

There were some very scary moments but there was also humour, as security forces overreacted to creative and harmless protests. Jaggi Singh, who had been arrested in 1997 in Vancouver at the APEC protest, was again arrested in Quebec, this time for employing a megaphone as a "weapon" and for being part of a group using an antique catapult to hurl teddy bears over the fence. He was held in jail for 17 days and went through a solemn trial at which Serge, one of the three very dangerous teddy bears who had made it over the fence, was produced as evidence of violent protest. Charges were dismissed.

Grannies in Quebec City sometimes didn't know whether to laugh or cry at the chaos; they had enough trouble finding each other and finding a toilet. It seems they had the same feelings we had in Seattle: confusion, fear, euphoria and guilt. Some Granny tactics seemed to work. They might have cooled a few hotheads on both sides, but the Grannies couldn't be everywhere. Could they have prevented protesters from throwing stones? Could they have bridged the gap between legal marchers and young activists at the fence who were easy prey for the police? What part should Grannies play in civil disobedience? The issue still hasn't gone away

In Victoria, all we could do was sing in solidarity with the Quebec City protesters at an anti-globalization walk that took the place of our annual Earth Walk. Then, when we heard about Jaggi Singh's teddy bears, we helped stage a protest at the Victoria courthouse with a mock fence and numerous flying, and deadly, teddy bears. Humour is more our style than stones, and maybe, in the end, it is the most useful protest we can make.

In the midst of all this furor, three Raging Grannies flew off to take Berlin. We were sent by Greenpeace to help persuade German pulp buyers to boycott forestry companies that were clear-cutting old-growth forests in British Columbia. For years, Greenpeace had been campaigning against this practice. This meant going to the buyers, wherever they might be, with a program of education, hoping this would stop the felling of B.C.'s heritage trees. It had been working very well in the U.S., especially with the publishers of newspapers and telephone directories, who liked to brag that they printed only on recycled paper.

Three of us, plus an honorary Granny, were to go to Germany: Fran, Freda and Ria, along with Shirley Langer from Tofino, whom Greenpeace had asked to organize the Granny part of this campaign. We wanted to do a good job, so we four had met in October and decided what we wanted in the way of songs and props. We even had Lina de Guevara, a well-known theatre director from Chile, now in Victoria, guide us with stage directions.

We decided to use Betty Krawczyk as our icon. She's an honorary Granny, an activist of Clayoquot fame, in her mid-70s, who had been defying the logging companies in the Elaho Valley by blocking their trucks, for which she was then serving the outlandish sentence of one year in jail. She was to be the rallying point for our crusade, and she went with us in the form of a larger-than-life silhouette that we put behind bars in a jail cell made out of plastic piping, all created by Ria. We also packed a 12-foot-high inflatable bear to represent all B.C. wildlife endangered by logging companies.

Thank goodness for Shirley, who functioned as a marvellous mother hen, reminding us to get our passports, buy travel insurance and acquire a black skirt and presentable attire — there was to be no bag-lady look on this trip. We also had to remember a good umbrella or raincoat and warm gloves. So, on a foggy December morning in 2000, we flew to Vancouver for a press conference with the local Greenpeace people and the media, who asked intimidating questions that would prepare us for anything that might be thrown at us in Germany. The press had just come from Interfor, the forestry company we were particularly targeting because of its insistence on clear-cutting old-growth forests, so they already had the company's side of the story.

Then off to Vancouver Airport for the flight to Munich. With her usual air of well-organized confidence, Shirley approached the check-in counter, four tickets and four passports in hand. The agent perused our tickets, our passports, our luggage, one after the other. Finally she did Shirley's, examining her passport, then handing it back to her, shaking her head. Our leader's passport had expired six months earlier.

We left her behind. When we had to change planes in London we got into more trouble. A British Airways officer asked if Shirley Langer was on board because her name was on the list of luggage in the cargo hold. We told him we didn't have her luggage, that she'd been delayed because of passport problems, but he insisted that the airplane had to unload all the luggage to make sure no unaccompanied bags were travelling on it. Then they had to X-ray our bags again. A long delay. We scrunched down in our seats to avoid the angry stares.

And when we landed in Munich, no luggage. We needed our stage props for our first performance the next day, and where was our mother hen when we needed her? Freda tried to cope with the lost-luggage forms in German, and Fran ran out to the waiting Greenpeace people and the press. With cameras rolling, her first words were, "Where are we staying and how do I say it in German?" Meanwhile, Ria, who spoke Dutch, made it very clear in the universal language of female insistence that our bags, including the *sehr grosse* (very large) box of stage props, had to be delivered to — what was the name of where we staying again? — before the next day. And they were.

Thank goodness we had Greenpeace to welcome us in Munich so we could do our show in the Winter Market the next day, with props that included the mock jail. We weren't sure anyone would understand our songs in English, so we used lots of emotional gestures and made sure the bear was centre stage. We visited the Canadian consul and tried to get him on our side while Shirley cooled her heels in Vancouver, waiting for the passport office to open on Monday. Our task was to tell as many Germans as possible what their companies' buying practices were doing to our forests. Most Germans love wilderness, and come in droves to appreciate ours, since even their Black Forest is a managed plantation now, so we had an eager audience. We were glad when Shirley caught up with us, because Greenpeace had lined up appointments for us with the chief executive officers of seven major paper companies and publishing houses in Munich. In Berlin, we met for an hour with the Canadian ambassador, the first woman to be appointed as ambassador to a G7 country. When she insisted there was little she could do to help, we suggested she worry about it before going to sleep at night, that her female ingenuity would find a way to save the forests.

We travelled on through Dachau, Augsburg, Dusseldorf, Hamburg, Berlin and then Hamburg again, singing to the Christmas crowds in the town squares. Greenpeace people were with us to ease the language barrier as well as to prime our conversation with the up-to-date facts. Our props helped a lot. The Germans were outraged to hear about Betty's incarceration, and they did like our bear. We were delighted to find that Greenpeace had a team of volunteers called the Over Fifties, who accompanied us from town to town and showed us around, besides helping us talk to townsfolk, the police and the officials.

Our reception at the German paper plants was not quite so rosy. We would be greeted by police, who probably expected us to take over the offices or climb a smokestack to hang a banner, since we came with Greenpeace; they have a strong reputation in Europe for putting their bodies on the line. Not even the consulates would admit the German Greenpeace forestry experts until we Grannies promised we would make them behave.

At company offices, we told the executives that the Grannies had a gentler approach than Greenpeace. We had come a long way to talk about what was happening to our wilderness and we wanted them to listen up. Were we successful? Hard to tell. We didn't make any sudden converts, but we did open their eyes to what their paper providers were doing to the wilderness of B.C. It was only later that we found out how much press our visit had generated. The Raging Grannies International website (www.geocities.com/raginggrannies) has dozens of articles and news reports in German.

The article we liked best came through to us in English via some sort of magic automatic translation device. We particularly enjoyed the biographical details of Fran, who apparently spent much of her childhood "upclimbing trees" but was now "moving" herself "nearly only with a bicycle."

Fran had lived briefly in Munich as a U.S. army wife in the 1950s and was delighted to see a wartorn city so beautifully rebuilt. She also noticed that dogs were allowed everywhere — in posh restaurants, beer halls, public transportation, fancy boutiques, large department stores, hotels and grocery stores. As our most fanatical dog owner in a gaggle deeply divided into dog-lovers and dog-haters, Fran returned to Canada with a new purpose: getting better dog access in Victoria.

Others among us were not going to join that dogfight. We had enough to do, battling politicians, especially the more right-wing variety that was springing up in the millennium. We were particularly anxious to get to Stockwell Day, the former auctioneer, logger, lay preacher and funeral-home employee who had been chosen leader of the Reform Party, which would soon evolve into the Canadian Reform Conservative Alliance Party, CRCAP. We were sort of sorry they had put "Conservative" in there and spoiled a good acronym.

We loved the photographs of Stockwell arriving at his first press conference in a wet suit, riding a Jet Ski. This man was set to go overboard, and we might be able to help him. So Alison, Fran, Anne and Betty hied themselves off to a barbecue being held in his honour at Victoria's Cedar Hill Golf Club, a public course. More than two dozen student protesters appeared on the greens with their own barbecue, for grilling organic vegetarian hot dogs, and some banners against people they considered bigots. We waited on the balcony of the clubhouse for Stockwell so that we could sing at him, though we can't remember now what the words were.

There was a noticeable stirring in the crowd. He had arrived. We craned our necks over the balcony, turned around again and there he was, right behind us, disappearing down the stairs to be swallowed up by the faithful. Next time we'll post a lookout.

The capper came as we were leaving and encountered a young mother on a nearby trail. "What's up?" she asked. We explained we were there for Stockwell Day. "What's a Stockwell Day?" she asked. Poor Stockwell's antics had evidently not caught everybody's attention.

We got a better chance at him in November 2000, when we snagged tickets to a Stockwell Day breakfast meeting at the posh Laurel Point Inn on Victoria's Inner Harbour. Fran, Alison and Ruth prepared to unfurl a banner denouncing the bigotry that we perceived among right-wing Alliance Party members. "Grannies against bigots," it read. Betty positioned herself on the other side of the banquet room to take photos. When Stockwell began his speech, the Grannies began to shout slogans and brandish the banner. Within seconds we were jumped by Alliance Party security guards, and the banner was torn from our hands as we were ushered outside. We didn't even get any breakfast, but the hotel security staff were so sympathetic they went back inside and retrieved our banner for us.

We didn't want to mention this encounter when we finally got to meet Stockwell Day on a road trip in September 2001, in a Princeton, B.C., coffee shop. Suddenly a familiar, shining face appeared. Could it be he? Anne went up to him and announced, with typical Granny tact, "Either you're Stockwell Day or you're his better-looking younger brother." He acknowledged he was the man himself, fresh from a talk to a high-school class. So we took the opportunity to lecture him on his enthusiasm for warmongering when the most-recent crisis in the Middle East was blowing up. Anne cited Winston Churchill and World War II. Betty urged him to be nicer to the prime minister. A few days later Day did start supporting our government's call for caution in following U.S. military, but not long after that the Alliance Party dumped him. A pity. He was such a nice target for satire.

A week after that Stockwell Day breakfast in Victoria, Prime Minister Chrétien arrived. Somehow, Ruth scored a ticket to the Coast Harbourside Hotel, but when she put on her Granny hat and began to ask questions, she was grabbed by Victoria's finest and hustled out, getting her protest on the front page in next day's *Times Colonist*. We're proud to know her.

Ruth Miller arrived to join the Grannies just when we needed her. She came with excellent credentials. She explains: "I've been a radical all my life. As a child I bullied the bullies at school and felt self-righteous about it, especially as I was backed up by my parents. When I grew older I joined the CCF [socialist precursor to the NDP]. I was a university-trained nurse, which required me to think for myself and to question authority, if directives did not seem to me to be in the patient's best interests." Part of her post-graduate education at Yale University included joining the Black Panthers. She took part in actions in Connecticut against racism, opposed the Vietnam War and demonstrated for daycare and affordable housing. Her peak experience was acting as marshal during a weekend anti-war protest in New Haven, Connecticut, when martial law was declared and the city was inundated by the National Guard. She came out relatively unscathed but was very shaken next day when the students at Kent State University in Ohio were gunned down.

Returning to Canada, she joined the Communist Party, was elected as school trustee in Kingston, Ontario, and ran unsuccessfully for the provincial government. She moved to Victoria as what she calls a streetwalker — a public-health nurse on the street helping mentally ill patients. "I knew many of my clients could not cash their disability cheques because they had no identification that a bank would accept. They were forced to go to cheque-cashing agencies that charged usurious rates of interest. So I regularly took them to my credit union and vouched for them."

Ruth still meets and greets her former clients downtown and recalls them with fondness, especially the woman who was in the habit of visiting Victoria's elegant downtown churches to wash her hair in the baptismal font. The only never-married Granny, for a time Ruth was also the most popular hostess for our weekly Granny meetings, which take place at various homes in turn. She lived for years on a boat at Victoria's Fishermen's Wharf, where she had a marvellous view and was in a fine position to hang out banners demanding peace and justice that caught the tourists' eyes.

But climbing up from the dock where her boat, the *Water Rat*, was moored could be fraught with danger, as she found out one night soon after her ejection from the Chrétien meeting. Down she went, into the drink, and was soon hollering as her winter clothes dragged her down and made it too hard for her to climb the ladder onto dry land. A neighbour called the cops, who aimed their flashlights and discovered her wallowing in the water. One of them announced, "Why, it's Ruth Miller." She was afraid they'd leave her in the water, but they relented and scooped her up. After all, they were Victoria police.

Ruth is also famous for having invented the creative shuffle, which is our answer when the police insist that protesters keep walking instead of standing and blocking the street. It works very well on the pedestrian crossing from the Fairmont Empress Hotel to the causeway. Following Ruth's example, aging Grannies are thereby able to stop traffic and get attention by proceeding ever so slowly across the street, political placards in hand. It can be done for hours if necessary.

We still needed reinforcements, largely because there was so much to protest in 2001, with sabre-rattling from the U.S. and service-slashing by the new Liberal government in B.C. We were losing Grannies because of physical or family problems, and the rest of us were feeling the pressure of too many demands and too many gigs. Doreen could no longer get to actions or to meetings because of her health; Ria had to spend more time caring for her grandchildren; it was hard for Laura to respond to calls for urgent action, living, as she did, on the other side of the Malahat, or for Freda to scoot in from Sooke, though they were invaluable with a little more notice. We needed new blood.

We had found, like most Granny groups, that 10 to 12 members is probably the best. More than that, and nobody has enough seats in her living room for our weekly meetings. And more than eight singing together can mean more than eight versions of a song if we don't keep together and watch our leaders, usually Fran or Anne, conducting with an elegant feather duster. But we can't afford to shrink. Fewer than 10, and we are scrabbling to find enough Grannies for a decent performance if times are busy and not everybody can get to a gig. Grannies do have other lives and other commitments. We needed new Grannies, but we've always been picky.

We've heard horror stories from other Granny groups who got stuck with stubborn power-seekers, or members who vetoed any action they didn't like. We'd been rubbing along together for years without formalities or serious confrontations and we wanted to stay that way.

Sure, lots of women want to join the Grannies. They accost us at performances or protests, begging to be let in, but we know from past experience that many wannabes want to wear the hats and enjoy the media exposure but don't want to do the work of lobbying politicians, researching issues, making signs, writing letters and planning protests. Not many of them realize that being a Raging Granny means a meeting every week and sometimes two or three protests or gigs a week, not to mention endless marches, carrying banners and then singing, often without a mike, to restless crowds. It also means being exceptionally tolerant, energetic and forceful.

So, how do you become a Victoria Raging Granny? You find us at a protest or through friends or via the library information desk. We don't advertise. A person's approach is important: too pushy,

Victoria Grannies Joyce, Anne Pask, Alison, Hilda, Mary and Betty (left to right) hit the high notes at this Unconvention in 1992 at Crescent Beach.

and we wonder why; too much a shrinking violet, and we know she won't stand the heat. Would-be Grannies need to show they are serious, that they have some sort of record as activists and that they understand what the Grannies are all about. It helps if they come recommended by a Granny gaggle or another group that we've worked with.

The next step is getting invited to a Granny meeting so that we can look each other over. One meeting is often enough to turn an applicant off. We are very noisy, very argumentative and even rude to each other. The energy level works just fine for us, but can be very intimidating to others. Cheerful insults abound. We don't go by Robert's Rules; we don't think he could teach anything to a Granny, anyway. We sort of believe in consensus, meaning that everyone has a voice: anyone can opt out of an action if she doesn't want to take part, and anyone can veto an action if she really and truly believes it is not in the Grannies' interest. That very rarely happens because there are few issues we disagree on. Abortion is one; assisted suicide is another. We can't remember any more. But even when we agree on an issue, we're mighty noisy. Everybody talks at once. The rotating chairperson makes feeble attempts to drive us through an agenda and we do take minutes, but if we had to describe our way of decision-making, we would have to call it anarchy.

A new applicant is treated much better than we treat ourselves; she's allowed time to tell us why she wants to join us and what she has been doing to change the world. Many applicants confess that they can't sing, which is fine, because we can't sing either. In fact, we are very nervous of those with choir or opera credentials because they would show us up. Nobody gets turned away because she cannot carry a note. Our lack of harmony is part of our charm, we're told, and we trade on it. If she is still interested after experiencing one of our usual chaotic meetings, and we are impressed by her potential, she is put on the waiting list. If she doesn't keep bugging us, she'll stay there. We admire persistence.

We don't care if an applicant is really a grandmother, since we're here to make it a better world for everybody's grandchildren, not just our own. We don't care about age; in fact we'd like to recruit younger Grannies who could stay the course better than some of us. We know of one Granny group composed of raging grannies and grandchildren, which sounds wonderful to us. We love it when our grandchildren come along to gigs but haven't got around to incorporating them into our group. We would like more youthful energy. The main difficulty in recruiting younger women is that work and kids do get in the way of Grannying, especially when so many protests and gigs come in working hours. So we are stuck with us crones. Most of us hate those dreadful euphemisms like "golden agers," although we do enjoy the cheaper movie and bus tickets and free BC Ferries rides on weekdays. We're not very comfortable with being "seniors" either, since that does imply a certain dignity, and to be an "elder" suggests far more wisdom than we could claim.

Since Victoria is so "white-bread," we've had very few applicants from other backgrounds, which is a pity, but not an issue we want to resolve by recruiting token ethnic Grannies. Mary Rose is the only one of us who was born in Victoria and we're a pretty mongrel lot, most of us being immigrants to Canada.

Our first new recruit in 2001, Sonya Ignatieff, came to us from a truly emigré family, first from revolutionary Russia and then from post-war Britain. And yes, she is related to philosopher-author Michael Ignatieff, although she deplored his support of the U.S. war against Iraq. "Lost causes have always been the rallying cry of the family," she says. Sonya provides a note of wacky elegance to the Grannies; she looks quite regal but she is a sucker for "in-your-face" action. We forgive her for singing in a real choir — the Gettin' Higher Choir — because she never criticizes the rest of us for singing so badly.

She brings a wealth of diplomatic skills, which are useful for representing us in a broad coalition that is trying to unite the Green Party and the NDP, and in meetings with community groups. While working for the federal government and as a single mum, she'd had to limit her activism to fighting developers who were trying to plaster her residential neighbourhood in Ottawa with 15-storey buildings. But her ire was bubbling below the surface, especially her anger at globalization, so she could hardly wait until she retired in 1998 and could join the Ottawa Raging Grannies. By that time her three children were independent and soon they headed west. That seemed a good idea for her, too, especially since she'd heard a lot about the original Grannies, of whom, she says, many other Granny groups across the country seemed in awe.

"How truly wild they were, I soon found out," she reports. "It was clear from my first ebullient meeting that these are women who speak their minds in a forthright and irreverent way so that no sacred cow is safe. Being part of them is serious fun." Even when it meant learning how to "rescue" each other from the police, in preparation for the G8 Summit in Alberta, Sonya has proved she can take on anybody.

Next came another experienced Granny: Wendy McDonald from the Edmonton "mob." We'd met her at several Granny Unconventions. While admiring the Edmonton uniform of poke bonnets, we couldn't help but notice Wendy standing out from the rest, her fake straw-yellow braids swinging from under the bonnet. We liked her nice style of anarchic choreography. Wendy was a ham. We knew she'd fit right in with us.

Her job as a public-health nurse in the area of family planning had turned sour when the Alberta government cut health care. She quit and joined the Edmonton Grannies. Like Sonya, she was lured to the west coast by her kids and immediately came to a meeting to see if she could join us. While we don't necessarily give preference to Grannies from other groups, we often find they fit well into our gaggle and we were delighted to have her. For a year, she hovered between Edmonton and Victoria, but then moved west for good.

Our latest recruit is Clara Halber. She got on our waiting list in 2000 and bugged us continually until we had to let her in two years later, and a good thing we did. Clara, barely five feet tall, is a little dynamo. Born in Cuba, she grew up in the heady time of the Cuban revolution in the 1950s. Her father was a school principal and the talk around the family table was always political. As a teacher, she worked in the literacy campaign that sent thousands of teachers and students to rural areas and resulted in an amazing literacy rate of over 90 percent. She also stood guard duty in the militia, though she never did get to use a rifle. She married an American in 1965 and they came straight to Canada. She had two children and moved 20 times, from Halifax to Inuvik, as her husband worked in various government offices from coast to coast. Clara got interested in community activities, especially the Women's Institute, and sang in a choir, but every time she became involved, she had to move again.

When her husband retired and was elected president of a Vancouver seniors' organization, she was drawn into seniors' issues. When both of them moved to Victoria, they found there was no longer a local chapter of the Old Age Pensioners' Organization (OAPO), though there were chapters all over B.C. In typical fashion, Clara decided to start one in Victoria, a chapter that would organize seniors suffering under the new Liberal government's cuts to services. Six months later, she was elected zone director of OAPO for the south island. We really thought that was enough work for her, but she insisted she had the energy to rage with us and nobody was going to tell her she couldn't find time to do both. So she joined us in January 2003.

We also have some honorary Grannies, like Janet Hawksley, Quaker and long-time peace activist, who is happy to join us if we need a crowd, and Jane Brett, who is an experienced campaigner against nuclear weapons, especially those on visiting ships. It's a delight for us when our "special agent," Diane Dobson, can join us. Blind, hemiplegic and diabetic, Diane is nevertheless a true Granny in spirit — a great activist for the disabled, an expert on their issues and a feisty fighter against governments of all stripes. When she wheels up for protests in her motorized chair, we have a hard time holding her back from mowing down the powers that be.

A dozen seems an ideal number for us. Any fewer, we'd be working too hard; any more, we'd fall over each other.

OLD FOLKS AT HOME

Sung to the tune of "Swanee River (Old Folks at Home),"
by Stephen Foster, 1851; lyrics by Alison Acker

Way down the waiting list for health care
Sadly we're stuck.
We're getting old and getting sicker.
Guess we are out of luck.
Old folks aren't a pretty picture
No one loves a crone.
Keeping us alive is too expensive.
Shut down the old folks' home.

Everybody loved the old Queen Mother
And kept her in gin.
The rest of us are seen as too much bother.
Someone should do us in.
When they write words on our tombstone
What will they engrave?
We're happy that you did not linger.
Thanks for the money saved.

CRY-INS AND DIE-INS

T o observe the millennium in 2000, we became a society under the B.C. Society Act, which cost us $100. Sometimes at our weekly meetings we anguished over things like slander, strategic litigation against public participation, known as SLAPP suits, and other legal challenges should one or more of us get carried away during a protest (such as the time Granny Joyce slugged a legislature security guard with a protest sign). It might follow that all of us were liable. As a society, we figured that if we were sued, the only assets to be grabbed would be a couple of hundred dollars in our Granny bank account, certainly preferable to having a Granny's house seized to pay a huge fine.

So we are now a society in good standing. Our stated purpose is "To dedicate our efforts to the children of the world so that they may live on a peaceful and harmonious planet, safe from war, injustice and pollution." Our first annual general meeting, required under the Society Act, lasted 10 minutes. Surely a record.

We were confident that our new standing as a society would get us special status with the B.C. Liberals, who had swept into office in 2001. The government had announced that it would dedicate part of Question Period to queries from citizens' organizations, and we intended to ask about the nuclear ships putting in to Nanoose Bay. However, the Speaker of the House declared that we were an unrecognized group, so our question was ruled out of order. We were tempted to ask for our $100 back.

Premier Gordon Campbell went ahead quickly with his election promise to hold a referendum on how citizens felt about treaty negotiations with B.C. First Nations. The First Nations were very upset at this, especially when they had a look at the questions. They asked folks to burn their ballots or otherwise destroy them. Grannies graced a ceremony of burning the ballots in a barrel outside the legislature, to support Rose Henry, a First Nations organizer and one of our local heroines. We joined her later at a feast and rally on the Esquimalt Reserve, where a flaming arrow set many more discarded ballots ablaze in a canoe. The referendum passed anyway, but the situation regarding land claims in B.C. is no further ahead and a good deal of acrimony persists.

Grannies have long admired Rose, a constant advocate for the poor and disadvantaged. Many of us donated money to help send her to the World Conference on Anti-Racism in Durban, South Africa, in 2001, and two years later she was to repay the favour by being the opening speaker at the Raging Grannies' Regional Gathering in Victoria.

Oil drilling off the B.C. coast is an issue we fret about too. We wrote to Ottawa when our provincial government threatened to lift the moratorium on it. There's nothing like little old ladies with no power, who know nothing about oil drilling, trying to influence government. Fortunately, Environment Minister David Anderson saw things our way this time and wouldn't hear of drilling off the west coast. That certainly pleased us, but today we continue to monitor the news. Imagine drilling rigs anchored off the Queen Charlotte Islands.

Still on the environmental theme, we were invited to the University of Victoria to perform and to meet Julia Butterfly Hill, a young woman who had just completed two years sitting in a 1,000-year-old California giant redwood tree, also known as a sequoia (several of them bless Victoria), to protect it from the landowner who wanted to log the area. It was a non-violent action in defence of the forest. Julia, the inspired daughter of a preacher, stood barefoot on the huge University Centre stage as she told how the Pacific Lumber Company had agreed to save the area and contribute $50,000 for scientific research. We sang a song to introduce her and left to the usual applause, punctuated by a sudden gust of laughter: Inger had to muster courage to return onstage and grab her skirt, which had fallen off. We were given copies of Julia's book as a thank you.

Valentine's Day 2002 turned up shortly after that, so we spent a creative hour or so at Anne's apartment and built a large, lacy Un-Valentine for Premier Campbell. We covered it with broken hearts. We invited the media to cover delivery to the premier's office, but none came. Reporters must have known that we wouldn't be allowed to deliver it to him personally. We had to leave it with the security guards and we have no idea if it ever found its way to Campbell.

Besides being upset at the province, at least some of us had a more local issue. The Greater Victoria Public Library Board decided to sell its Esquimalt branch to McDonald's. Betty and Inger, who live nearby and use the library a lot, were outraged. The problem was that Alison was the Esquimalt representative on the library board and had recommended the sale. It was a strange thing for her to do since she held such adamantly anti-globalization views.

Betty and Inger helped organize a loud local protest, but it was a done deal, part of a complicated local political tempest in a teacup that certainly led to the defeat of many sitting councillors in the 2002 election. Once Alison's term on the library board was over, Inger and Betty could laugh with her about it all, but they still accuse her of choosing hamburgers over culture.

We could all agree on the need for improved health care in B.C. When former Saskatchewan premier Roy Romanow came to town on his Canada-wide tour to hear presentations on the state of our health-care system, we couldn't address him personally, but we were able to sing a few songs about medicare to an amused camera group taking video evidence. We were assured that yes, the boss would listen to our words. We were not as confident that B.C.'s Premier Campbell was taking our Granny advice as seriously.

Our first chance to show our displeasure with him was in February 2002 at the official opening of the B.C. legislature, which coincided with a student protest over the threatened increase in tuition fees. We joined a pretty young crowd, mostly students, 4,000 of them, who assembled to holler, shout catcalls and boo. The flimsy fence erected to keep out the barbarians at the Legislative Buildings was soon lying flat on the ground. The police had the sense not to overreact. Some of the young people refused to leave and erected a mini tent city on the rain-soaked legislature lawn, calling it Camp Campbell. It was still there in its sogginess on February 23, when more than 10,000 people arrived in a fleet of buses from the Lower Mainland and the islands to protest the proposed Liberal budget cuts and plans to privatize everything from hospital laundries to major highways.

It didn't take long for activists, street people and transients of all stripes to move in, making the most of the donated food, warm clothes and Arctic-ready tents. Some nights, temperatures fell below zero. Grannies brought food and money, blankets and warm clothes, took photographs, chatted. Alison and Fran gave a civil-disobedience workshop emphasizing the peaceful aspects of democratic persuasion.

The squatters dug a vegetable garden on the legislature lawn, outlining it in stones configuring the yin-yang symbol. One protester expected to see lettuce and onions by the summer. After all, he reasoned, they were camped on First Nations territory and he didn't care how many injunctions the attorney general got to throw them off—it didn't matter because the First Nations would allow them to stay.

The attorney general did get an injunction. Serious activists went home to sleep in warm beds. Idealism declined. Marijuana smoking increased. Bare-breasted women danced across the lawn and a television cameraman got socked in the face by a protester, who was promptly arrested. In the fading afternoon light on a grey day, Grannies were on hand to stand guard as the police watched over the dismantling. The campers helped load debris onto municipal garbage trucks. Within days the lawns were reseeded, the hopes of a summer veggie garden only a memory.

We didn't want to get damp and cold to protest the holes in B.C.'s social safety net, but we did want to have our say about welfare. Murray Coell, the provincial minister responsible for social services, had reneged on a promise to meet us, and suddenly he announced a plan to slash welfare. It was no accident that we chose April Fool's Day to remonstrate. Since it was also Easter Monday, we brought the Easter Bunny with us. The rabbit was on his way back to his Saanich lettuce patch, coincidentally right near Coell's house in suburban Victoria, and would leave an empty Easter basket on Coell's doorstep.

We were apprehensive about reduced welfare payments and the new law that forces parents on welfare to return to work when their child reaches the age of three, whether or not the mum can afford daycare. Our hand-painted sign said it all: "Do Liberals Really Care About Kids?" The local TV audience saw it on the evening news. Another sign offered advice: "How to Balance the Budget: Tax the Rich Corporations. Stop Robbing the Poor."

The media arrived about the same time as the police. The cop remarked, "It's just the Raging Grannies," and left after ensuring that we were on public property. Ruth, wearing pink bunny ears to match her pink T-shirt and fluffy white tail, delivered an empty Easter basket to the front porch of Coell's townhouse. And there she was on the five o'clock news. Of course there were letters to the editor, even an editorial, deploring demonstrations at a politician's private home, especially by those appalling Raging Grannies. Somebody else, though, defended our action, calling our critics grouchy.

The next month we got really cheesed off with the B.C. minister of health and his budget-paring and decided to do something serious about it. After much plotting, we met at a restaurant near the Ministry of Health building in downtown Victoria. Mustering our courage, we casually sauntered into the building. Anne dawdled behind with Laura's cell phone, alerting the media. Ostensibly we were there to view a collection of paintings in the lobby; in truth, our intention was to stage a "cry-in."

At a signal from Fran, we grouped at the front entrance, lay down on the floor and began to cry at the top of our voices, handkerchiefs to our eyes, which were streaming with tears from

On April Fool's Day/Easter Monday 2002, Anne Moon, Fran, Sonya, Alison, Laura and Ruth (left to right) enlist the help of the Easter Bunny to protest slashes to the social safety net.

laughter. The racket we were able to make for nearly an hour totally surprised us. The acoustics in that building were made for a protest. The foyer rises several storeys high and the noise, we learned later, mounted and reverberated throughout the entire building. Since it was lunchtime, we attracted lots of attention from the incredulous staff going in and out of the building.

The security guards, of course, called the police. However, a newspaper reporter arrived first, with a TV camera not far behind. Unfortunately, by then the guards had locked the outer doors and we couldn't communicate with the media. We should have left one Granny outside to explain our protest. And since we thought it unwise to issue a news release before our action, the press didn't have a clue why we were on the floor weeping and kicking up such a fuss. The police finally arrived. They told us they would either drag us out and arrest us or we could leave on our own and go home. We chose the latter.

"Am I going to get a record?" quavered Anne in her best little-old-lady tones.

"Not with your voice, you're not," quipped the smarty-pants sergeant.

Fran and Freda were able, briefly, to make our case to the TV cameras about the sad state of B.C. health care by continuing the wailing and weeping as we left. A picture of Freda crying her eyes out graced the Victoria *Times Colonist* the next morning.

The police, as they escorted us outside, thanked each of us for leaving so peaceably. Anita, one of our octogenarians, chose to take the proffered arm of the law to steady her retreat; the rest of us declined. Anita loves to remind us, "If you're not living on the edge, you're taking up too much room." Despite this advice, Anita always uses a pseudonym when she calls the phone-in program on CFAX, one of our local radio stations. What this achieves we often wonder, since anyone who knows Anita would instantly recognize her cultured voice.

We have tried to keep a good rapport with the local police. Anne or Ruth compliments them every time, by phone or in

In 2002, Fran (left) and Freda are escorted away from the Ministry of Health after a "cry-in" staged in the foyer, where acoustics were perfect for a protest against health-care cuts. (DEBRA BRASH/VICTORIA *TIMES COLONIST* PHOTO)

writing, when they do the right thing by not overreacting to a dicey local situation over the homeless folk or the street folk or peaceful protests. We believe that if policemen act responsibly, they will be respected.

Victoria police were not so polite with six women who occupied MLA Jeff Bray's office. The women, who called themselves the Kimberly Rogers Womyn's Brigade after an Ontario woman who died while under house arrest for welfare fraud, were dragged out by the riot squad. With about a hundred sympathizers gathered, including a small number of Grannies, police got nervous and pepper-sprayed three young women who were sitting in front of the police van. It was the first time Victoria police had used pepper spray on a group. Their tactics raised quite an outcry and alerted the Grannies that cops can get nasty with young folk. Could we have protected them? We're still not sure. Charges of vandalism against the group were dropped and they all got off with a promise to do community service, which the kindly judge agreed they were doing already. All our MLAs beefed up their security, which included new gates guarding the legislature.

We continued to make our displeasure known about the provincial government. Ruth dropped in to a Victoria Chamber of Commerce meeting at the Fairmont Empress Hotel, where Premier Campbell was guest of honour. She reported that nobody could get into the hotel lobby that day, though there were lots of protesters outside with signs and songs who heckled the MLAs as they arrived. One staff member who was blocking Ruth from the entrance said, "I'm only doing this because it's my job."

Still on the issue of health care, Alison got the Grannies involved in the newly resurrected Victoria branch of the B.C. Old Age Pensioners Organization, which was suddenly trying to get pensioners excited about politics. Late in 2003, Inger, Clara and Betty helped to write a skit with other members of the OAPO and performed it at a party called "stop the burnout" for health-care workers. The skit was about the inequities of seniors' health care.

Since most of us are seniors, we can empathize with those whose lives are fading away. Our meeting minutes constantly reflect that fact. Unhappily, that makes our minutes somewhat boring, but occasionally there is a bit of a sparkle.

At one meeting, the minute-taker recorded a *good* regular Thursday meeting. We never rate meetings. They are all good. However, in this instance the meeting was judged. Why? Among the 19 items on the agenda was "we discussed our sex lives!" And that was it. No interesting tidbits were recorded. Senior memories being what they are, none of us can recall what we talked about. Sorry.

Sometimes we talk about death, too. A couple of our Grannies belong to the Right to Die Society and we either squirm or laugh nervously when they describe such contrivances as the plastic "exit bag" that a friend can zip over your ailing head when the going gets too tough. One of our Grannies even purchased a contraption for blowing up balloons with helium, thinking that it might be easier to use than carbon monoxide from car exhaust. These right-to-die folks are creative in a deathly sort of way. We reminded her of helium's explosive nature and talked her into returning the item and putting her money to better use, like a bottle or two of Scotch or a joint of marijuana when the need arrives.

Our discussions about death often move into genuine distress over what is happening to health care in our province. No matter how hard we tried, or cried, government ministers refused to meet us. Campbell's government was about to increase both drug costs and dispensing fees for seniors, adopt a modified means test and who knew what else directed against the poor, the sick and the disabled. We thought this quite unfair of them, so one October day in 2002 we met outside the legislature and synchronized our watches for a serious protest within the House. We entered the visitors' gallery in three groups: Fran and Freda; Alison, Ruth and Inger; Laura and Anita. Betty sat in her car nearby with Laura's cell phone. At the designated time she phoned the legislature press gallery and advised that a bunch of cranky old ladies would be yelling "Affordable health care for everyone" at the end of Question Period.

While Grannies in the gallery were awaiting their opportunity to yell, they were treated to testimony on MLA health care. A number of the MLAs had lost weight by diet and exercise over the past few months, and now they were busy congratulating themselves on the reduction in pot bellies all round.

Finally Question Period ended. Fran and Freda stood up and shouted "Affordable health care for everyone." Betty was watching closed-circuit TV in the legislature rotunda and heard the shouting, but then the sound was cut. Upstairs, security guards hustled Fran and Freda — still shouting their mantra — out of the gallery. Immediately Alison, Inger and Ruth took up the cry. They too were bundled out. That left Anita and Laura, who carried on with the message. Betty, meanwhile, got out her own camera and ran up to the gallery, only to be told to "get out of here." As she retreated downstairs she was gratified to pass the media racing up, laden with cameras and tape recorders.

She watched as Fran and Freda, followed by Alison, Inger and Ruth, were rushed down the stairs and across the rotunda, still mouthing off to the press as they were marched through doors marked PRIVATE DO NOT ENTER, where they were lectured severely. Finally Laura and Anita appeared in the rotunda, escorted by two women guards. Laura was feeling faint, and they allowed her to slip away, then the two guards disappeared. Anita felt honour-bound to follow the flow through the DO NOT ENTER doors. She pushed open the door, only to return when no one there paid her any attention.

Within minutes a number of security guards materialized in the rotunda. They told the curious members of the public to leave immediately; the legislature was closing. They were concerned that not all the "terrorists" were accounted for. They only had five in custody and there were supposed to be six, or was it eight? Goodness knew where they might be hiding!

Later that afternoon the Grannies were reunited for a photo shoot for the *Vancouver Sun*. Betty told the gang to smile; the camera guy said, "No, don't, look angry." Without hats, and scowling, we looked like fugitives in the resulting photo. The accompanying headline read: "Grannies Shout Down MLAs and Shut Down the Legislature."

The news report quoted Alison Acker, 74, saying, "They're not listening to the people," and Fran Thoburn, 70, complaining, "Hospitals are being closed." None of the Grannies was charged, not even with disturbing the peace. However, all five were banned from the legislature. To date none has "officially" been back.

The result of this disturbance was increased security at the legislature at a cost of $200,000. Even Victoria's *Times Colonist* grumbled about the unnecessary expense of keeping people away from the halls of power:

> [They've] dug trenches in the immaculate lawn in front of the Legislative Building to accommodate ugly gates … to make it as secure as the U.S. Embassy in Beirut.
>
> Mr. Speaker and members of cabinet who also have offices in the buildings are not concerned with suicide bombers. The people they want to keep out are the poor, union members, social activists, peaceniks, tree-huggers

and Raging Grannies. In short a good sampling of the people who live in this province.

Iron bars and TV cameras aren't necessary to protect the government from disaffected citizens. All Richmond [the Speaker] has to do is turn on the sprinklers on the legislative lawns. Works every time, and it's cheaper, too.[1]

In May, just months after being banned, Inger did try to attend a hearing at the legislature on BC Hydro privatization, but when the security guard found out her name he wouldn't let her in. Early in 2004, three of the banned Grannies had their luncheon orders cancelled and were hustled out when guards spotted them in the legislature dining room. Well, if B.C. wasn't happy with Granny protests, we decided to see how social justice protesters fared next door.

In June 2002, Ruth, Sonya, Freda and Alison went to Alberta to protest the G8 Summit at Kananaskis. Actually, we went to Calgary, because security staff kept everybody miles from Kananaskis itself. The G8 is an informal group of eight countries — Canada, France, Germany, Italy, Japan, Russia, the United Kingdom and the United States — which discusses matters pertaining to the World Bank, the International Monetary Fund, etc. It's a big deal. International terrorism has been on the agenda, along with drugs, international crime and any wars or conflicts then in progress or about to be launched.

Our quartet went trembling. The Quebec fracas and other police-bullying tactics in Europe had been shown widely on TV, and who knew what might happen in Alberta? We Grannies had survived some scary local workshops on civil disobedience put on by members of the Ruckus Society. Though based in Oakland, California, they seem to turn up when required to provide "environmental and human rights organizers with the tools, training, and support needed to achieve their goals." We learned how to free anyone arrested, how to snarl bodies with chains or tubes so that the police couldn't get at them and how to protect limbs from batons and lungs from tear gas.

After the Battle in Seattle and the Quebec confrontation, which Sonya had attended, we expected the worst. Alison bought a gas mask. The rest of us read what information was available on how to deal with tear gas. But there was no need for gas masks or eye washes. The protest organizers had learned a lot about how to get their message out, and in Calgary they created an alternate summit called the G6B People's Summit, named for the six billion global citizens.

We travelled in comfort in Ruth's Volkswagen van, waving demurely at the military caravans we passed. We found the heat our worst enemy; the temperature reached 34 degrees Celsius in Calgary.

We didn't attend many of the alternate summit teach-ins. You can't teach old dogs new tricks, and we didn't think we needed much more education. We went to *do* something: to point out to the world how politicians and multinational corporations work together to manage the masses. We wanted the world to understand that a chief executive officer of a large corporation has more money at his (invariably *his*) disposal than most governments. The bottom line in corporate endeavours is usually profit — profit at any cost — which means companies too often close factories in the developed world, throwing thousands of workers out of jobs, and reopen in the underdeveloped world, paying wages two-thirds lower. Our presence in Calgary had to do with direct action and solidarity with like-thinking activists, hoping to make the world a more equitable place for us all.

At the first protest gathering, a sweet-faced, very large guy from the Anarchist Black Bloc promised to "rescue" us if we got arrested. We weren't really reassured. We joined a long march that continued until sunset. It ended with a "Show Down at the Hoe-Down" outside the more ritzy gala at the Calgary Stampede grounds, where the city's elite was hosting G8 delegates.

The next day saw us up at 6 A.M. to join a dawn peace ceremony, where Granny Jean McLaren and Starhawk, icon of environmental and political Wicca, blessed everyone. We needed it indeed, because the snake march through Calgary lasted for hours, totally exhausting us. But everything was peaceful. Our scarlet-and-white Granny banner got a rave reception and we gave interviews "on the hoof" to media from as far away as Germany.

The organizers of the Calgary protest were keeping us all too busy and too tired to do anything serious to disrupt the city. These were two days of peaceful protest at its best. The weather was hot and the cops were cool. Police officers on bicycles looked on as we put "sorry to inconvenience you" signs on the windshields of cars held up by the march. At another intersection, when faced by an aggressive gang that wanted to push down the barricades, the cops merely moved the barriers aside and stood back. That afternoon we were delighted to lie down at last for a "die-in" at a downtown park. We collapsed on the concrete while imitation vultures swooped above, and a priest gave us what we feared were the last rites. That was okay with us. We were worn out.

In Calgary in 2002: Hot and tired after a hard day's protesting, but still smiling, are Victoria Grannies Sonya, Alison and Ruth.

Then up and on, to a park on the other side of Calgary where Calgary and Edmonton Grannies were singing. We got there just in time for the last two songs. Bone-weary and barely standing, we squeezed into a concert by Bruce Cockburn and finally staggered to bed, guests of a Calgary sympathizer who couldn't protest herself but wanted to do her share.

We did get to a couple of workshops, but the knitters among us were sorry to miss the "revolutionary knitting circle," which was symbolically striking a blow against sweatshops by a return to traditional crafts. The braver ones regretted arriving in Calgary too late that first day for a back-to-nature demonstration involving a lot of mud and bare flesh.

We left Calgary overjoyed by demonstrations that didn't descend into violence, either by our side or theirs. Nobody got to Kananaskis. The nearest any protester got was to the highway turnoff, where they were met by the Canadian army. But we did make a difference in Calgary by chatting up every citizen we met to talk about globalization and why we were protesting. We were relieved that there was no call for either gas masks or lemon juice to counteract tear gas.

We got home in time for our yearly Hiroshima remembrance ceremony in early August. Often, international students come from the Lester B. Pearson College of the Pacific to make peace lanterns to float in the tidal waters of the Gorge Inlet. Someone plays haunting music on the flute; someone else reads Japanese poetry. And when it is all over, Fran and her partner Hub go out in their canoe to collect the stray lanterns. It is always a meaningful, peaceable evening.

On Remembrance Day, most of us wear white poppies to salute peace workers as well as to remember the civilian men and women killed in war. We make our own white poppies and some of us wear both red and white.

It seems there are ever more wars to remember now. As a result of the terrorist attack in the U.S. on September 11, 2001, we have seen war in Afghanistan and Iraq. The conflict in Israel and Palestine continues. There is enmity and atrocity in much of Africa. Some Grannies agonize mostly about international events, others get mad at local politicians. We try to "think globally and act locally," rather than watching TV and wringing our gnarled aging hands in despair. It saddens us that there are more wars to protest than we ever imagined possible, and we weren't pleased that Canada, as a member of NATO, was compelled to send soldiers into Afghanistan.

In August 2002, before the war in Afghanistan began, we joined a die-in at the Department of National Defence recruiting centre in downtown Victoria. Police rerouted traffic away from the one-way street as the march trailed through the city. At the sound of an air-raid siren from somebody's tape recorder, we fell to the ground. It was eerie. The media took pictures and a couple of people drew outlines in chalk around our bodies, reminiscent of a homicide scene.

Although we were distressed by the terrorist attacks in the U.S., we did not think bombing Afghanistan was acceptable. However, on September 20 President Bush declared war on terrorism, and on October 7 the bombing of Afghanistan began.

In Victoria a Wednesday-evening peace vigil was started at the foot of the cenotaph at the B.C. legislature, initiated by the Victoria Peace Coalition and the local branch of the International Socialists. The first vigil drew over 200 people to the legislature lawn. There were many speakers. The legislature security guards began taking photos, and since some of the speakers were Muslim, the organizers, who sensed a possibility of racial profiling, put up umbrellas to make it more difficult for the cameras. We carried signs: "War Never Again," "No More Wars," "Let's Declare Peace," "Say No To War," "Quakers for Peace & Justice," "Bread Not Bombs," "War Kills Kids," "Disarm Now," "Honk for Peace."

The second week, 50 people turned up. As the weather got colder and wetter, there were only 25 and sometimes as few as four or five.

Honorary Raging Grannies Jane Brett and Janet Hawksley went most Wednesdays, as did Alison. The rest of us turned up sporadically. The weeks leading up to the Iraq war were very cold, wet and windy, and few old bodies could take more than 15 minutes of that.

The war memorial features a World War I Canadian soldier holding his rifle high, bayonet at the ready. Most passersby, folks on bicycles, in cars, trucks, even tour buses, supported the ongoing vigil by honking their horns, waving support or stopping for a chat. We like to remind our American visitors of what Benjamin Franklin said: "There never was a good war or a bad peace."[2]

The Wednesday-evening peace vigil continues as of this writing, even though some well-meaning souls ask, "Don't you know the war is over?" The response always is, "Which war?" The vigil closes as we hold hands in a circle and sing "Go Now In Peace."

The legislature guards, many of them old soldiers, don't bother the peace people anymore. In fact, they wave at us each Wednesday, and some even drop by for a chat before we leave.

To contend with terrorists at home, such as the ones who steered airplanes into the World Trade Center in New York and the Pentagon in Washington, the United States passed a new Patriot Act and fashioned new security measures. Many human rights and personal freedoms were suspended. We decided to remove the U.S. from our travel plans because of what looked like racial profiling. Many innocent Muslims were arrested, tarred with the same brush as real terrorists. By January, Taliban fighters captured in Afghanistan were hustled off to an American military base at Guantanamo Bay in Cuba and held, not as prisoners of war, but as detainees in legal limbo, without charge and in appalling conditions. Canada implemented security measures too, but none as draconian as our neighbour to the south.

During most of 2002 it was apparent, despite the on-again, off-again inspections for weapons of mass destruction in Iraq, that another war was imminent.

As if to challenge Canada, on September 20 the USS *Nimitz*, an aircraft carrier capable of carrying nuclear weapons, arrived off Victoria. Normally these are informal visits and the immense decks are empty, but this time they were bristling with warplanes. Betty took a digital photo and sent a copy to Prime Minister Chrétien and Foreign Affairs Minister Bill Graham, saying, "The USA may be preparing for war, but hopefully Canada has more sense than to follow suit." We did our usual demonstration downtown, but the visiting sailors kept their distance. These were tricky times.

Meanwhile, the Israeli–Palestinian conflict continued. A couple of us attended a demonstration at the Spanish civil war memorial in downtown Victoria during the height of the intensive Israeli response to Palestinian suicide attacks. It was an attempt at rapprochement between several groups in the city. It didn't appear to be very successful, but at least it was peaceful. (Raging Granny Jean McLaren from nearby Gabriola Island has been three times to Palestine as a peacekeeper, under the auspices of both the International Women's Peace Service and the International Solidarity Movement.)

As the rush to war with Iraq continued, Scott Ritter, an American ex-Marine and ex-UN weapons inspector, came to the University of Victoria to speak to a packed house, which included most of us Grannies. Ritter disagreed totally with his president's hurry to wage war, claiming that there were no weapons of mass destruction in Iraq.

On February 2, 2003, the Canadian frigate HMCS *Rainbow* left Esquimalt for the Middle East. It was not off to the impending war — it was part of the UN mandate to impose sanctions on Iraq — but we used the occasion to oppose the looming war. Alison had created another banner reading "Say No To War." Four of us, on a cold, wet, windy day, dressed as warmly as possible and stood on the seaside cliffs to display the banner, defying hundreds of Victorians who had come to wish the ship Godspeed.

We would make good use of the "Say No To War" banner over the next few weeks. Several times we hung it over the Trans-Canada

Highway for the morning commuters to see. That, too, is a cold and windy place, and we always wore gloves and scarves and our warmest socks. It was gratifying to receive honks and hand waves in support.

On February 15 massive peace protests were held around the world, but the invasion of Iraq began anyway on March 20, led by the U.S. and Britain. It was a short war. Aboard the aircraft carrier USS *Abraham Lincoln* on May 1, President Bush declared an end to major combat operations in Iraq, but six months later peace had not yet come to Iraq.

In August, Betty wrote to the Victoria *Times Colonist*:

Yes, democracy may be the best political system available today, but it cannot be brought about by bombing a populace into submission.

It is absolutely unconscionable to destroy the infrastructure of a country and then let out contracts to your buddies to rebuild it. America may not be imperialist, but boy-oh-boy are they ever the supreme capitalist state working for the shareholder not the citizen.

And don't forget there were no weapons of mass destruction, the reason for attacking Iraq was just not there.

The bombing of Iraq was aggression pure and simple.[3]

As hostilities against the occupying U.S. soldiers grew more and more serious in Iraq, Americans became even more protective of their homeland. A strategy known as the United States Nuclear Missile Defence Shield — a newer version of Reagan's Star Wars — surfaced. This so-called missile shield would deploy American missiles to shoot down incoming nuclear weaponry before they crossed into the United States. That meant most inward-bound missiles would be blown up over Canada.

We decided to take seriously the suggestion made by the Center for Strategic and International Studies in Washington that Canadians should request government funding for hardhats, since "having missiles intercepted overhead is something Canadians will simply have to live with.

"Missile debris will hit Canada … it's Canadians who will have to deal with the debris from destroyed enemy rockets raining down on them. The Pentagon needs little from Canada for its proposed missile shield — except the air space in which to blast apart incoming missiles … Canada might want to request extra funding for hardhats, but there's not much else that can be done about it."[4]

It was time to encourage citizens to get their own hardhats, rather like those gas masks the Brits carried around with them during World War II. We even put an advertisement in the newspaper for surplus hardhats. Alison collected an assortment from a military bloke who had read about our protest and, surprisingly, agreed with us. He wanted to remain anonymous. Fran painted the hardhats with glowing flora and fauna. Betty printed out information cards, and off we sallied to Clover Point. That's where the yearly Swiftsure sailboat race in the Strait of Juan de Fuca begins, and we strutted our stuff at the regatta's pancake breakfast. Looking fetching in our hardhats, we sang, "Missiles keep falling on our heads" to the tune of "Raindrops Keep Fallin' on my Head."

Folks didn't appear too concerned. It was a divinely warm day in May. The pancake breakfast was scrumptious. Multitudes of dazzling sailboats were massed on the sparkling water, ready to set sail out into the strait. All seemed right with the world. One well-dressed gentleman in tweeds and tie took exception to our endeavour. He ripped up our information card, glaring at us with fire in his eyes. We carried on with a clear conscience. We had done our best to warn the citizenry of possible impending doom. Even Environment Minister David Anderson, who was selling breakfast tickets, admitted to us that he found it hard to defend a plan that would see our country put at risk in order to save U.S. cities.

We have a bit of a history with David Anderson. Some years earlier, he was behind a long table, flipping pancakes for spectators watching the start of the Swiftsure race, and as usual, Grannies were there in full regalia to make a statement. Anderson spied his nemesis, Anita Bundy. "Not you again. This is a day for fun, not politics," he quipped. But Anita continued to brandish her huge yellow sign stating, "Warning, nuclear ship now in port," because that very day there was a U.S. nuclear-powered ship in Esquimalt Harbour.

A few months later Anderson went to the CBC radio station downtown to answer questions on its noon phone-in program, got out of a taxi, saw Freda, Inger and Anita in hats and boas — ever fierce protectors of the CBC — and sneaked around to the back door. On his way out he was not so lucky. Anita caught him and he had to stop and listen to her because people gathered on the street were watching. So he smiled a rather sickly sort of grin.

At one time he held an open house in his office. Six Grannies in full dress awaited him. Betty dumped into his hands a six-kilo package of petitions that demanded increased funding for the CBC and made him promise to deliver them, in person, to the prime minister. At that point most of us dived into the tea, cakes and even sausage rolls. Eventually we left, except for Anita, who continued to bend his ear, on and on, until the few constituents who were left gave up hope of talking to him and disappeared too.

Weeks later Anderson came to town with a cheque for the new Blanshard Community Centre. Grannies took over the front row, but since we had come incognito, security was merely suspicious. Anderson expected a great day, handing out a million dollars, almost as if it was his own money. But Alison, Inger and Anita bombarded him with questions, and Inger had brought her tape recorder. Our questions encouraged others to ask difficult questions. Anderson managed a strategic retreat, but we still have him in our sights; at the time, he was the only cabinet member on Vancouver Island.

Sung to the tune of "(Oh My Darling) Clementine,"
Percy Montrose circa 1880 or traditional; lyrics by Alison Acker

With so many women telling
How Bill Clinton dropped his jeans.
After fifty years of silence, we're about to spill the beans.

Chorus: It was chilling, it was thrilling,
It was such a romantic fling.
Though we blush when we confess it,
We all slept with Mackenzie King.

He was lusty but somewhat dusty
And he liked to play leap-frog.
He kept talking to his dead mother
But he really loved his dog.

Chorus

We've been waiting for successive
Prime ministers to ring.
Diefenbaker? Or Mulroney?
Maybe Paul would like a fling.

Chorus

GETTING BIGGER AND BETTER

Women power is a formidable force.
— *Dr. Gro Harlem Brundtland*

For years we have been attending the Remembrance Day ceremony at Nanoose Bay, where the nuclear submarines play. Initially it was a long walk. Now, we park our cars nearby, have a ceremony and are scarcely noticed by the guards at the gate of the Canadian Forces Maritime Experimental Test Range, operated jointly by Canadians and Americans. We trust, however, that a message about our peaceful presence gets sent to both Ottawa and Washington.

Despite the appalling international news in 2002, Grannies had lighter moments, too. Our Christmas party was held on Ruth's spectacular boat at Fishermen's Wharf. We always loved our meetings there, getting dizzy when her home rocked from the wake of passing boats and having to shout over the roar of a seaplane landing nearby. But to actually go below decks and have all 12 of us able to sit down — with elbow room — at a resplendent antique dining table was remarkable. Sadly, it was our last gathering there, as strictly enforced zoning rules and higher fees forced Ruth onto dry land.

Several Grannies in their Granny gear went as usual to the New Year's Day levee at Government House. A levee is an assembly held by a sovereign or her representative at which, by tradition, only men were received. In Victoria, the New Year's levees involve much of the citizenry. At several municipal levees, delegations of the homeless and the poor have appeared to sample the repast. Raging Grannies, except for Betty, who was appalled at the effrontery, even attended a levee at the officers' mess of the Royal Canadian Navy in Esquimalt. However, Betty did approve of the Oak Bay levee where they served sherry. Esquimalt always provided the best food, but apparently a new council plans to downgrade future munchies.

After the Government House levee, Ruth reported that she had a meaningful discussion with Iona Campagnolo, the lieutenant-governor, who was receptive to Granny concerns. Some months later Alison, who had also chatted with the lieutenant-governor, was again at a posh function at Government House, this time representing the Greater Victoria Public Library Board. Campagnolo claimed not to recognize Alison in civvies.

Meanwhile, on Vancouver Island some brave women were waging their own war in the woods. Women in the Woods superstar Betty Krawczyk (an honorary Raging Granny) and Jenn Bradley were put in jail for challenging B.C.'s forestry policy by picketing logging operations in Vancouver Island's stunning old-growth Walbran Valley. After her arrest, protesters designated a huge Douglas-fir tree as Grandma Betty.

Grannies had already sent pithy notes to the premier about the B.C. Liberals' plan to allow much more of the province to be logged. Perhaps local writer/activist/TV host Briony Penn put it best. She was the star turn at our 2003 Granny Regional Gathering in Victoria, where she warbled, "Take our trees, we'll never use them; take our fish, we'll only lose them; you took the part that once was our heart, so why not take *all* of B.C.?"

We had felt obliged to host a Gathering because it was well past our turn, and we hoped that hosting the smaller regional meeting would spare us from having to run a larger Unconvention. A Gathering is a mini-Unconvention within a finite geographical area: in our case British Columbia, Alberta, Saskatchewan, Washington, Oregon and California. Unconventions are a much bigger deal, now held every two years, and drawing Grannies from all over the continent.

Gabriola organized one of our first Granny Unconventions, which were held every year to begin with. As the movement spread and there were more groups across Canada, we changed to biennial Unconventions and Regional Gatherings in between. The first Unconventions took place in B.C. because that was home. They were more intimate meetings than later ones because there were fewer of us. Alison remembers swimming in the nude on Gabriola Island, hoping that the faithful spouses cooking dinner for us couldn't see. The Victoria Unconvention at Glenairley retreat in Sooke in 1990 also included swimming — but this time in the freezing Pacific Ocean and in swimsuits, because we didn't want to upset the nuns who run the retreat centre, although they upstaged us by staying in the frigid water for half an hour while we merely jumped in and out, quickly.

Salt Spring Island hosted the next Unconvention, which had us sleeping in a yurt, toe to toe, and then singing at the Ganges market. Vancouver has hosted us three times. One year we sang to great applause at the Granville Island Market and then bought some nasty-smelling dried fish that we mailed off to the prime minister to protest some federal action about fisheries, though now we don't remember what it was all about. And then Vancouver hosted a very successful Unconvention on Bowen Island, which brought in new Grannies from Alberta and Washington State. At the same time, Vancouver became so busy that three groups were flourishing there to keep up with the demand. The growing protest against provincial cuts gave rise to the Raincoast Grannies, devoted especially to the environment, and the Gastown Grannies, responding to social issues, while the original Vancouver group tried to cover everything.

Unconventions both united and widened the movement, drawing increasing numbers of Granny groups to Toronto, Lethbridge, Edmonton, Halifax, Kingston and, in 2004, Ottawa. Every Unconvention has brought in newcomers anxious to start their own group and has fired up veteran Grannies who were feeling battle-worn.

A Granny Unconvention is noisy. It always includes a mass protest, such as the Toronto Unconvention's invasion of the Pickering nuclear-power plant, which was so accident-prone it was proving a threat to most of Ontario. It got targeted by a horde of Grannies infiltrating the more usual and more polite groups of visitors and asking pointed questions.

One Granny pounded on a locked door. "You can't come in here," the security guard told her.

"Who would want to, with all that radiation?" she sniffed.

Every Unconvention also includes information on issues such as globalization, workshops on songwriting, street theatre or passive resistance, "show and tell" entertainment when each Granny group performs recent skits or songs, and a very brief business meeting to decide who gets to host the next Unconvention and who will publish the next issues of our newsletter, *The Grapevine*.

We're not much into business or philosophy. Sometimes we argue about whether or not to incorporate to protect our name or to mount national campaigns, but we pride ourselves on not taking ourselves too seriously, even at Unconventions. We don't take minutes; we rotate the duties of chairperson; and we never, ever refer to Robert's Rules of Order. Unconventions are for swapping songs and experiences — and sometimes hats — for chatting about what works or doesn't work and for simply getting together. We rarely let insiders watch or listen, and we don't want mainstream press, except when we organize a group protest. At Unconventions, we want to let our hair down, even if it is grey.

All of us worked on our 2003 Victoria program, though Anne came up with the most innovative ideas. She corralled speakers, organized the bus, even became quite dictatorial when necessary. Freda handled the registration, Fran was the banker, Sonya dealt with St. Margaret's School, where we were gathering, and set up the classrooms and the reception area. Betty bought the wine and the soft drinks. Laura collected the wine glasses, the little plates and the napkins. Wendy and Alison organized the collection of guests from ferries and planes. There were early-morning Tai Chi sessions and brisk hikes to a neighbouring pond.

We got a real boost when Victoria's alternative newspaper, *Monday Magazine* (which inexplicably publishes on Wednesdays), put a bunch of us on its cover the week before the July gathering. The upbeat article about what we are doing these days was an auspicious start to a successful get-together.

Keynote speaker Briony Penn arrived on her bicycle next morning, bubbling over with enthusiasm. Briony is an eco-warrior in the media world, trying to convert from within through her column in *Monday Magazine* and her environmental reporting on the New VI-TV in Victoria.

"Well," she began, "you Grannies may be the opposite of eco-goddesses." She must have been comparing us to the younger eco-women who tastefully graced the 2001 Salt Spring Island calendar in their collective buffs in order to raise consciousness about the environmental danger menacing their island. Most of us remembered Briony's famed Lady Godiva ride along Vancouver's Howe Street that helped bring a stop to logging on part of the island. Wearing nothing but a wig and underpants, brave Briony rode a horse through the city's corporate canyons until the president of the Texada Land Corporation agreed to halt his chainsaws.

Briony told us that Raging Grannies had been around for centuries. Her slide show had coloured sketches of an Egyptian Granny with hieroglyphics deploring local environmental abuses. A Greek Granny carried a PAX sign. Okay, so she wasn't a linguist, quipped Briony. A Roman Granny, in a toga, was obviously involved in an anti-poverty rally. A Jewish Granny, looking suspiciously like the Virgin Mary, sang about safe sex, as evidenced in lowered eyes and a Bible. Mona Lisa was certainly a Granny, arrested trying to save an old-growth forest — that resigned look on her face, you know. The French artist Monet was protesting the threat of nuclear fallout: his wife carried an umbrella. Then came Picasso. His grumpy Granny made up of cubes and squares really knew what was what. Picasso got it just right. Well, he had many a Raging Granny lover, didn't he?

EGYPTIAN RAGING GRANNIES SAVING BIRD HABITAT/WETLANDS
IN 1200 BC-NILE BLOCKADE

CARTOON BY BRIONY PENN

ARRESTED FOR TRYING TO SAVE OLD GROWTH

RENAISSANCE GRANNY

CARTOON BY BRIONY PENN

The day carried on with workshops on networking, keeping peace in Palestine, non-violent communication, how to make protest props and plotting an actual street demonstration. That evening was devoted to performances from the 17 gaggles present, along with a warm welcome to an original Granny, Bess Ready, who was sprung for the evening from her suite at Oak Bay Lodge.

The next morning 61 of us got on a chartered bus for a scenic tour and a demonstration. The sight of Raging Grannies protesting in downtown Victoria at 9:30 A.M. was a rare treat for early-bird tourists. We more than surprised the Fairmont Empress Hotel as we milled about its green lawn, objecting to that damned American missile defence plan. Although we figured the venerable hotel was solidly built and safe, there was no room at the inn that day for Raging Grannies with anti-Star-Wars placards.

We descended on the legislature, asking for a tour on behalf of the Americans among us. No luck. So we staged a brief die-in in the shade. The shadows were welcome, as Victoria was experiencing a rare heat wave. We strolled back to the bus, fell exhausted into the seats and drove past more spectacular scenery, feeling very pleased that the sky was so clear and the Strait of Juan de Fuca and the Olympic Mountains so lovely to behold.

Our destination for lunch was Pearson College, and when we arrived, much to our amusement, our host informed us that he had just received a phone call from the RCMP warning the college of the impending arrival of those dangerous Raging Grannies.

"We know. We invited them," said David Skilling, the college's information officer. We wondered who the mole was and were awed by the fact that the Mounties had the time to make the call.

Our Victoria Regional Gathering at St. Margaret's School was a success. We got only two complaints — too much good food and not enough free time. Well, we can live with that. There was no plenary, no chairperson, no resolutions, no policy setting. Our next stop was Ottawa for a National Unconvention in May 2004.

The Internet has sure made it easier for us to round up the troops for protests, letter-writing campaigns and Unconventions. As in the rest of the world, communication among the Raging Grannies has exploded. We thought we were high-tech when we got telephone-answering machines. Now we are into mobile phones and Palm Pilots and posting pictures on the web. Even our most confirmed, outspoken Luddite, Alison, recanted and joined the 21st century when she got a computer and an e-mail account.

Betty was the first to be captivated by the challenge of the computer. Freda was next, encouraged by her son, a computer whiz. Inger surprised us by buying an IBM and learning how to use it in jig time. Fran shows great promise. Anne came to us already well versed, as did Wendy and Sonya. The others need and accept help. Fortunately, computer crashes are more easily overcome these days. Betty has upgraded and dumped six computers over 10 years and almost as many printers, modems, scanners, zip drives and sound systems. However, Anita still throws up her hands in frustration and Ruth gets glassy-eyed when the talk at meetings goes on too long about creating address books and firewalls.

Initially, our news releases were hastily typed after enthusiastic, fervent telephone conversations had determined who, what, when, where and why. One of us would go to the cheapest copy place for a bunch of duplicates, and drive around to the radio, TV and newspaper offices to hand out our breathless bit of stop-the-press journalism. In those days Betty's enthusiasm about the nuclear submarine threat often resulted in a well-researched, three- to-five page essay that might have got her a C- in history and an A in sociology. But the media didn't care about why. What was news was what these wintery old dames were up to now. So she shortened the news releases to one page and eventually to one line.

By 1995 Betty had acquired a telephone/fax for 50 bucks, set it up and was able to save on gas by pushing news releases through the fax slot. We can fax *el presidente* of Colombia, or the president of the United States, too, if they get up to something we disapprove of.

E-mail is a curse and a delight. Today, all of us but Anita communicate by e-mail, amending letters we jointly send to politicians or reminding each other of a commitment or a date for lunch somewhere. We can even critique a new ditty written by Alison.

Inger was the first to purchase a cell phone, thinking it would be cheaper than a MedicAlert bracelet. Betty was the first to get a Palm Pilot, but keeping it in batteries proved too expensive. Now she too has a cell phone but refuses to give the number to the rest of us.

Raging Grannies touch base two or three times a year via our newsletter, *The Grapevine*. Betty learned more about what she and her computer were capable of achieving during her three years as editor than anything else she's dabbled in. But, oh man, what a roller-coaster learning curve.

The first issue crashed her computer when it ran out of memory, so she ended up cutting and pasting. The second issue, on a new computer, crashed the hard drive (fortunately still under warranty). *The Grapevine* was late, but with the new computer's expanded memory, she could e-mail the entire 16-page issue to anybody whose e-mail server would allow it. Eventually she was able to include pictures from an anarchist web page of the Battle in Seattle, including photos of participating Grannies. At the Free Trade in the Americas protest in Quebec City in 2001, several Grannies were able to pass pictures back and forth and Betty posted several onto the Independent Media Center, an alternative news site.

Granny Robyn Smith edits *The Grapevine* currently, out of Vancouver. Her dedication is to die for, but it's getting hard to keep up with all the Granny happenings these days across the country. Both Ottawa and Toronto have Raging Granny websites so we can keep abreast of worrisome issues and share protest songs with many new gaggles.

We never meant to start a movement. It grew on its own, like a weed, and we couldn't be more delighted. Search engines show hundreds of references to Raging Grannies and their activities in Canada, the United States, the United Kingdom and Australia. There is even a gaggle in Athens, Greece, nourished by Grannies Philippa Jecchinis of Toronto and Mary Mantis of Minnesota. No doubt there are others, Grannying away unrecognized. Being Grannies, we never agree on how many groups of Grannies are now in action, but it is somewhere around 70. We are all too busy to keep count.

The movement grew by example. Victoria is such a popular tourist destination that visitors were bound to discover us and pick up the idea. The more media exposure we got, the farther our message spread. The growing gap between rich and poor in Canada and the U.S., as governments swung to the right and became more belligerent, was sufficient to rouse protesters seeking a new and more effective way to get their message across.

The first groups to follow Victoria's lead were our close neighbours, Salt Spring Island, Gabriola Island and Vancouver. They saw us in action and got inspired.

Salt Spring Islanders Lorna Pentz and Virginia Newman were at that 1987 uranium protest, saw the Victoria women performing and said to each other, "We can do that." They formed the second Granny gaggle one week later, choosing to appear as elegant ladies dressed in garden-party hats, long black skirts, white T-shirts and gloves, with added beads, shawls and parasols — outfits designed to contrast with their clever songs. The Raging Granny icon with the upraised umbrella, used on their T-shirts, was created by Art Simons, the husband of Granny Marg Simons on Salt Spring Island.

Ever since, they have been singing at the famous Ganges Saturday Market-in-the-Park, carrying their portable keyboard with them as they move from stall to stall and hand out fact sheets with background information on whatever issue inspires them. They are also proud of their work in schools, which has included a tour of elementary schools through the Fraser Valley.

Also at that 1987 rally was Jean McLaren, of Gabriola Island: "I saw some elderly ladies (like me) dressed in very proper clothes, a bit old-fashioned-like, maybe from Value Village, but they had on hats with flowers and were carrying handbags a lot like those belonging to the Queen — not the kind you can pack your lunch and some leaflets in or maybe your toothbrush and a change of underwear in case you were arrested.

"They climbed onto the platform and started to sing to the tune of 'Daisy, Daisy,' but with lyrics protesting those nuclear subs. Right there and then I said, 'I want to be one of those' and went home to organize the Gabriola gaggle.

"I never knew how powerful Grannies were until I was in Palestine in 2003 with an international group working for peace. I was stuck at a checkpoint with people who had been waiting for hours just to get home. An Israeli soldier with a big gun asked me what group I was with. I told him 'The Raging Grannies.' He laughed so hard he nearly dropped his gun and let us all through."

Not all groups operate in the same way, and not all groups are large ones or busy ones. Some small ones are very effective because they take on local issues and they know their audience. One of these is the Raging Grannies of B.C.'s Sunshine Coast, who have to deal with the disadvantage of relative isolation in small towns separated by difficult roads. The group began with just five women and has wisely followed the advice "Think globally, act locally." They have concentrated on local environmental issues that are part of the global picture: drinking water, forestry practices, the saving of public land from the forestry giants. In spite of feeling remote from mainstream actions a ferry ride away, they have sung their messages to visiting Ottawa politicians at a fisheries conference, in high schools, in malls, at union gatherings and at women's rallies. Even when the group dwindled to three stalwarts, they kept going until new, younger women joined. As Helen Roy, one of the originals, says, "We are there when needed, and we will always be there, hopefully with more of us."

Next to appear after the original B.C. burgeoning were groups in Ontario. Toronto led off on a bitter November day in 1989, headed by Betsy Carr. Their protest against NATO's fighter bombers training over unceded lands of the Innu in Labrador was blown away in a howling gale. Phyllis Creighton, a music and song enthusiast, joined and now their songbook has 300 entries. In May 1999, three of them went to The Hague Appeal for Peace meeting in The Netherlands, where they sang to an audience of 2,500 with thousands more watching on jumbo TV screens outside the theatre. The video of that night is still touring Europe. Then they went back home to face provincial Ontario policies and homelessness, poverty and diminishing medicare.

Kingston joined in when the Bread and Roses caravan for women's rights crossed Canada in 1991, bearing news of the rising tide of Grannies. Rose DeShaw was running a rare-book store at the time and getting tired of writing letters to the editor. "Grannying sounded like a godsend," says Rose. "I went to a songwriting workshop attended by a few high-powered singers brought together in this choir town. By the end of the session I'd done 15 songs and was madly scribbling another but nobody else had written a word because they wanted perfection. I waved around the first Granny songbook [put out by the Gabriola Grannies] and pointed to the pictures: 'Look at these women. What counts isn't great singing. It's having a sense of the ridiculous.'"

Rose visited Hamilton and helped start a gaggle there. She went to a protest in Toronto, carrying with her Granny Gertie, Kingston's life-sized doll in frilly chiffon with pink, fuzzy slippers, who gets chucked around and then rescued at protests. Rose took Gertie to Queen's University where Paul Martin, who was finance minister at the time, appeared in an expensive suit with no bodyguard. "I found myself gently poking him in the tummy with the rubber chicken I always carry. There's a picture of us both looking down, with the chicken firmly ensconced in his belly button."

The Ottawa Grannies, known as the Parliament Hill Mob, sprang up in 1987 to protest a weapons trade show, but faltered until the '90s when Virginia Cameron and Alma Norman, in full Granny regalia, sang at a send-off for the protesters' train heading for the Clayoquot Sound showdown in 1993. They'd brought along spare Granny hats and co-opted two other Grannies, one of whom was Ottawa's then-mayor, Marion Dewar. The Ottawa Mob are kept on the hop, living as they do "in the belly of the beast," and the focus of national attention. They're great at street theatre. One Earth Day they wriggled their way down Sparks Street wearing a giant earthworm costume and, of course, singing an earthworm song.

They're also game for protests out of town. This is how Peggy Land, a Quaker Granny with the Mob, describes her experience at the Quebec City protest in 2001: "We sang our songs composed for this event with great gusto and were often cheered and hugged along the way. In our outlandishly colourful hats and shawls, we were happy to put a face to those of "mature age" who felt just as outraged as the younger protesters with what was being cooked up by the various heads of state inside the fence. But maturity brings its self-appointed responsibilities, of course. So when clouds of tear gas were seen rising from the fenced-off areas above us, some decided to go and show solidarity with the younger folks. The Grannies made a more-than-symbolic left turn and headed up the steps towards the freshly tear-gassed area, despite warnings from fleeing protesters.

"Soon we came across a group of heavily armed police in full combat gear. They looked more like armadillos. One armadillo stepped forward, fingering his rubber-bullet gun. Undeterred, the group linked arms and put themselves between the small group of protesters and the police. First they sang and then they took small steps towards the police. Then it was 'We Shall Overcome' and a few more steps forward, voices cracking a little. Finally, Alma Norman, 78 and tiny, explained to the police that they could indeed be their mothers or grandmothers and it was the same for the protesters, but they were simply there for peaceful purposes and posed no threat.

"Amazingly, the police retreated a few steps and stopped. The Grannies blew them a few kisses and made their way back down the hill to much applause from the protesters and then joined other Grannies for the official march."

Brantford, Halton County, London, Peterborough, Woodstock, the Blue Mountain region and Simcoe County all caught the Granny bug. Kitchener–Waterloo got into action in a typical fashion: They had an issue — threats of pesticide use on the verge of a public highway. Somebody had heard of the Victoria Grannies' protest songs, so in January 2000 a few local women produced songs and signs and gathered 40 protesters, including some men who called themselves the Grumbling Green Chorus. They became the news of the day and have gone on to further actions, most of them to protect the environment.

Ralph Klein's right-wing Conservative government in Alberta helped spread the movement there to Edmonton, Lethbridge, Calgary and Red Deer. Soon, Regina was fielding 14 Grannies and five daughters. Next came Saskatoon.

In B.C., the movement spread east across the mainland. Pat Grinsteed of Kelowna was featured in her local paper, putting out a call for Grannies, and they appeared as if by magic, many with valuable experience from working on women's issues. Very few groups have been able to incorporate men or even to inspire Raging Granddads, but some have recruited daughters or granddaughters, which seems to work fine.

At least two groups have teddy-bear members. Elaine, a teddy in green velvet cloche, blue-green shawl and peace pin, commemorates Toronto Granny Elaine Hall, who died in 2000 and goes along on their gigs. Joyce Lydiard, a long-time force behind the Vancouver Rainforest gaggle, died early in 2002 and was reincarnated as Teddy Bear Joyce, bravely taking on the G7 at the Calgary protests that summer.

When Montreal became a Granny stronghold back in 1989, they were determined to encourage a Francophone group. Les Mémés Déchaînées came together in 2001 and have sung many times, alone or with their Anglophone sisters. That was the year the Montreal group was awarded the YMCA peace medal. Montreal has also become famous for its fashion show. Grannies parade down the runway, showing off the clothes; then they read the labels, which reveal that most of the garments are made in sweatshops. It's a show that other groups also perform, though we believe that Montreal does it with the most flair. As a follow-up, they launched a campaign to persuade the federal government to change textile-labelling laws; they want labels to include the names of contractors and subcontractors so that we can know what we are buying and whose sweat produced it.

Windsor evolved into Grannies Without Borders, linking with the Detroit Grannies in 2002. Patricia Lay-Dorsey of Detroit put out a call and reported, "Fifteen women showed up at my door and agreed to perform the following Sunday at a Windsor anti-war rally." Some were members of an earlier Detroit group that had foundered for lack of members. They borrowed their first songs from the Rochester, New York, Grannies, who are now one of the largest groups anywhere, with 70 members.

Soon, Grannies Without Borders was tackling the U.S. government for its war on Iraq, the Detroit Water Board for cutting off water to more than 40,000 homes for non-payment of water bills, the Immigration and Naturalization Service for its racism and the local malls for selling war toys. Then they defied the coldest day of the year in Washington, taking foot-warmers along for the march of half a million people against the war in Iraq. In her regular e-mail journal, Patricia relates: "I drove down, taking my scooter, and met our charter bus and 13 of the Rochester Grannies. I had to run interference, calling out, 'Make Way for the Grannies!' One of our Grannies ran out of steam and had to stop walking, but a man happened to be pushing a cart with cardboard boxes piled high and he let Maggi climb aboard and get a ride ... We were the last ones on the march and police on motorcycles tried to shoo us up onto the sidewalk, but we figured we had as much right to stay on the streets as everyone else so we just kept on walking."

Rochester Grannies got even luckier. They were boosted on board a flatbed truck and rode all the way, singing Granny songs. Also on board was Granny D. Haddock, aged 93, who had walked coast to coast across the U.S. in 1990 with a message of peace and justice. They also met Grannies from Hamilton, Ontario, and from Chapel Hill, North Carolina, and gave out lots of cards to women who wanted to start gaggles in their own hometowns.

Grannies have also sprung up in Phoenix, Arizona, and in Vermont (thanks to Lanie Melamed of Montreal, who, sadly, died of breast cancer in 2003) and in Palo Alto, California, where the Peninsula group has about 30 Grannies, many of them Unitarians or Quakers and many of them veterans of Vietnam War protests. They use a frying-pan tambourine, kazoos and washboards and even boast an accompanist who plays an accordion, Dana Marie

St. George. They also dance, and they have sung with Joan Baez. We're all jealous.

"Our first confrontation with local police was in June 2002, when we demonstrated our displeasure with the Bush administration as Condoleezza Rice [President George W. Bush's national security adviser] addressed the graduating class at Stanford University," says Granny Ruth Robertson, one of the Palo Alto gaggle. "The sheriff tried to move us away, citing our use of the word 'bomb' in one of our songs. We pointed out that the lyric was not 'bomb' but 'missile' and the exchange became heated until a *San Francisco Chronicle* reporter showed up just in time to prevent our expulsion. Since then, we've had great press, being called everything from 'an elderly women's chorus' to 'a punk band of warbling wild women.'"

Seeing the Peninsula Grannies in action inspired a new group in Sonoma County, California. Carol Hince and Canadian-born Mimi Wright contacted Canadian groups, downloaded Seattle's protest songs, posted flyers around town and by December 2001 had enough recruits to sing fractured anti-war-toys carols at a downtown mall.

Seattle Grannies first appeared on February 12, 1996, after hearing Victoria Grannies perform at Seattle's Northwest Folklife festival in May 1995. We still laugh about that gig. What were five Grannies doing, looking for a drugstore at 11 P.M. in Seattle? Searching for condoms, that's what. We needed them for our song about safe sex: "Hey ho, hey ho, it's off to bed we go." It would be nice to have them in colour, so they would show up better when we brandished them. The drugstore clerk didn't bat an eyelid and the audience at the festival loved us — and so did the watching wannabe Grannies in Seattle.

"We began as groupies," says Kay Thode, also Canadian-born and one of the Seattle originals. "Then they invited us to sing with them and finally they left the stage to us." The Seattle group numbers 20, and many have sung together in the Seattle Opera chorus — an accomplishment that awes many vocally challenged gaggles such as Victoria. But they are not mere entertainers. They've taken on city council, the local school board, hearings in Hanford about reactivating a nuclear reactor and, of course, the U.S. rush to war in Iraq, and they take great heart from the cheers of young people chanting, "Go, Grannies, go!"

We were surprised to find Grannies in the United Kingdom and Australia, by searching the web. In April 2003, women based in Exmouth, Devon, showed up in London at the largest demonstration in 20 years — a protest against Britain's participation in the Iraq war. Mo Mooney, the Exmouth organizer, explained to a reporter that getting out on the street empowered them to act after years of quieter protests as part of local churches and peace groups. They then took to the streets of Exmouth, doing a "knees-up," though in full Granny regalia. Next, three of them got arrested blocking access to an Esso gas station, to protest what they called "a war for oil." It all began with an article on the Canadian Grannies in Britain's *Saga Magazine* in 2001. Though the Exmouth Grannies do not appear to be connected with any other gaggles in Britain, we suspect others have also sprouted.

We have no idea how the movement spread to Australia, but by July 2001 Raging Grannies were protesting visits to Australia by U.S. Secretary of Defence Donald Rumsfeld. They were particularly incensed by the establishment of the Pine Gap Joint Defence Facility, 20 kilometres from Alice Springs in the Australian outback. A mass demonstration in October 2002 included protesters of all kinds, from the Sydney Tennis Players Affinity Association to Grannies for Peace. One Granny, Dorothy Buckland Fuller, aged 80, travelled for three days to get to the protest. A sociologist by training, she deplored the U.S. disregard for Middle East culture and the creation of a missile facility that infringed on the sovereignty of Australia. The Australian Broadcasting Corporation featured the Grannies for Peace, with their huge sunflower banner and sunflower aprons, marching to the Alice Springs courthouse, where some of the protesters were arrested.

With so many gaggles, *The Grapevine* has proved a wonderful instrument of solidarity and a healthy source of debate. What should we do about members who object to any criticism of Israel or any personal fault-finding of a politician or the occasional Granny with a bee in her bonnet about abortion or fluoridation? Our general advice is to ignore them. Grannies with very divergent views usually quit.

There was the famous Granny uniform controversy in 2002. Some Montreal Grannies were upset upon observing photographs of the Boston group wearing our trademark flowery hats, but otherwise dressed in normal street attire — in fact, incomplete Grannies, in their eyes. Fran, of the Victoria group, countered in *The Grapevine* as follows: "If the Boston tribe wants to protest by simply donning hats, that's okay. If another group wants to wear bonnets and aprons, that's fine by me, too. Originally we adopted a look that parodied the little old ladies you see on our streets — dark woollen overcoat with fur collar, patent leather purse, dowdy hat, pink running shoes. But now my favourite attire is a pair of tights and a top with spangles of all colours that clash marvellously with the red boa and the blue insects on my hat. Skirts and shawls get in the spokes of my bike. Aprons are for the kitchen, where I spend as little time as possible. Who cares? It's our hearts and our courage that make us Raging Grannies." She added a postscript: "Betty Brightwell has reminded me of the time we appeared on the main street downtown wearing bikinis (with hats) to draw attention to the depleting ozone layer, and Ruth Miller brought up our decision to seriously consider appearing nude (with hats) should we feel an issue desperately needs attention."

Indeed, there is a rumour that some members of our group unbuttoned their shirts in 2003 for Victoria's Second Activist Olympics, organized by a gathering of left-wing friends, exposing their breasts — solely, of course, to illustrate the problem with George W. Bush. Obviously he lacked the milk of human kindness, and we could show what he'd been missing. The Woodstock Grannies took their own way round a similar issue by singing about a Guelph woman who won the right to go topless in public, ending the song by opening their shawls to display fake boobs made of stuffed nylon.

Then came the age controversy that kept the e-mail humming for weeks in the fall of 2003. The Kelowna group innocently reported that they were preparing new Granny guidelines, which specified an age limit of 55 or over in order to preserve the Granny image. This led to a barrage of protests from Grannies under 55, including Cathy Hamel. Cathy, a member of the Woodstock, Ontario, gaggle, is known as Hamgran and keeps us all in touch through e-mail. She learned about the Grannies from a fellow member of the Canadian Auto Workers Union through her nighttime job in a welding shop. She has three children, one a teenager, but is still in her early 40s. She sensed ageism and promptly quit. We had a hard time enticing her back. Gaggles rethought their rules and it appears most of us agree that being a Granny is an attitude and not a question of age.

But the navel-gazing continued. Other groups appeared to have been busy for months with guidelines, rules and mission statements and were anxious to share them. One gaggle rashly announced that their group alternated "leadership," which aroused many a protester, including Fran, who reminded everybody that Victoria Grannies have always insisted that every Granny is a leader. And we never have bothered with much of a mission statement. We strongly believe Grannies can be trusted to know what to do and we'd better use our energies to do it instead of arguing about aims and objectives.

The spate of e-mails gave some of us a sore finger from pressing the delete key, but our e-vine is a wonderful way to keep in touch. Most groups are "wired" and proud of it. Betty has mastered digital photography, to get our actions instantly posted on the Independent Media website (www.indymedia.org). This way we can make it round the world without having to battle newspaper and TV outlets that become less and less willing to feature any protest against the status quo.

There is a directory of groups and of some individual Grannies, but we are sworn not to pass the lists around. A number of groups also have their own websites, the Ottawa site designed by web-Granny Corinne Allan being the most resplendent of all. Corinne also designed and runs our Raging Grannies' International website. Victoria hasn't yet got that far. It would take more effort to keep up to date than any of us is willing to provide.

Now that we're getting so widespread and well known, some Grannies have been pressing to incorporate our name, just in case somebody appropriates our image and name for commercial use or to push for some cause we don't all believe in. We were shocked to see that one Raging Granny link on the Netscape browser leads to a site advertising "mature horny women." We're still in the process of getting incorporated, and never realized how difficult it would be. A few groups, like Victoria, are registered as societies, but we're not sure that being a society gives us much protection if somebody tries to sue us for slander. We just hope they wouldn't want to look so silly. A lawsuit might be kind of fun.

Being a society means we have to remember to have an annual general meeting and re-elect ourselves to our board of directors. We do have a minute book so that we can check up on the things we promise to do, though we're never very sure who's got the book. At each weekly meeting, somebody different gets to chair and somebody else gets dragooned into taking minutes — except for Alison, who is too pushy as chair and has such bad handwriting nobody can read her minutes. Fran, our treasurer, actually keeps books, though our only income is the loonie a week that we drop into a Granny piggy bank. It's enough to pay for printing leaflets, etc. We don't seem to get honoraria anymore, perhaps because we don't go in for entertaining, but more likely because our singing is so awful.

We hate to think we are settling down now that we don't have to make so many road trips. To practise our togetherness, we take short trips, sleeping too many in a room and still arguing over who snores the loudest. The same old problems persist. For instance, the dog dilemma. When we visited Doreen's cottage on Galiano Island, east of Vancouver Island, Chinook, Doreen's Tibetan terrier, was so incensed by the intrusion of Fran's Bernese Mountain Dog, Molly, that she peed in Molly's food dish. And Inger, who can't stand dogs, is always the one who gets fawned and slobbered over. Whenever we plan a trip, somebody asks, "Are you bringing that dog?" and the arguments start. Age should bring tolerance, shouldn't it?

We're much easier about husbands. Usually they clear out as soon as a Granny gathering is threatened. It's amazing how much gardening a husband can get done when Grannies are around. Since most of us have shed our menfolk through death, divorce or general disagreeableness, we try to be very nice to the remaining husbands. Andy Gibson, husband of Salt Spring Granny Betty Gibson, creates clever songs in the style of Gilbert and Sullivan. Other husbands are vital in providing transport to and from the ferry or airport, and they usually have their own busy lives to lead. We know we're lucky that any men put up with us. The wise ones try politely to ignore us. Husbands come and many of them go, but the Victoria Raging Grannies show no sign of fading away.

We are mindful of Emily Carr's observation: "It is not all bad, this getting old, ripening. After the fruit has got its growth it should juice up and mellow. God forbid I should live long enough to ferment and rot and fall to the ground in a squash."[1]

When we can no longer climb into kayaks or haul ourselves up the steps of the legislature, you may find us trading in our rockers for wheelchairs, forming a cavalry to charge down Government Street, going the wrong way, of course, with the tips of our umbrellas sharpened and at the ready.

And when we finally kick the bucket, just think what ornery angels we'll make.

ENDNOTES

CHAPTER ONE: IN THE BEGINNING
1. *The Globe and Mail*, January 10, 1989.

CHAPTER TWO: FINDING A VOICE
1. W. Jackson Davis, *Nuclear Accidents on Military Vessels in Canadian Ports: Site-Specific Analyses for Esquimalt/Victoria*, Nuclear Policy Program, Adlai Stevenson College, University of California at Santa Cruz, October 15, 1987.
2. *Focus on Women*, August 1989.
3. Audrey Thomas, "Oh Victoria!" *enRoute*, April 1989, 40.
4. *Edmonton Journal*, August 21, 1989.

CHAPTER THREE: ALL AT SEA
1. *The Martlet*, October 12, 1989.
2. *The Martlet*, October 19, 1989.

CHAPTER FOUR: TEA AND NO SYMPATHY
1. Jim Gibson, "Our Town," *Times Colonist,* January 1990.
2. *Ottawa Sun*, October 7, 1998.
3. *Times Colonist*, November 2, 1990.
4. *Times Colonist*, November 10, 1990.
5. Letter to the Editor, *Times Colonist*, January 1991.
6. *Esquimalt News*, January 9, 1991.
7. Letter to the Editor, *Times Colonist*, January 6, 1991.
8. *Times Colonist*, January 13, 1991.
9. *Times Colonist*, November 29, 1990.
10. *Times Colonist*, November 29, 1990.
11. Anita Vidal, *Monday Magazine*, December 27, 1990.
12. Joshua Handler and William M. Arkin, *The Neptune Papers, No. 5 Nuclear Warships and Naval Nuclear Weapons, 1990: A complete inventory*, September 1990.
13. *Times Colonist*, November 17, 1992.
14. *Times Colonist*, December 31, 1992.

CHAPTER FIVE: ON THE ROAD, THROUGH THE WOODS AND INTO TROUBLE
1. *The Province*, April 13, 2000.

CHAPTER SEVEN: WAVING THE FLAG
1. Peter Grant, *Victoria from Sidney to Sooke*, Altitude Press, 1994.
2. *Chatelaine*, October 1991.
3. *Fifty Plus*, Canadian Association of Retired Persons, October 1999.
4. *Maclean's*, December 30, 1996.
5. Dorothy L. Sayers. (Sir Impey Biggs in *Clouds of Witness*, 1926).
6. *Maclean's*, December 30, 1996.
7. Warren Magnussen, "Critical Social Movements: De-centering the State," in *Canadian Politics: An Introduction to the Discipline*, Broadmead Press, 1990.
8. Nicole Tate-Stratton, in *British Columbia Woman to Woman Magazine*, January 1993, 16.
9. *Saga Magazine*, August 2001.
10. Marcia McClung, Nellie McClung's granddaughter, says, "Family lore claims she said it on a train when someone was overheard criticizing her."
11. Speech to the United Nations General Assembly, May 26, 1978.

CHAPTER EIGHT: FOREIGN AFFAIRS
1. Vaclav Havel, Speech to a joint session of the House of Commons and the Senate, Ottawa, April 29, 1999.

CHAPTER NINE: CRY-INS AND DIE-INS
1. *Times Colonist*, April 7, 2003.
2. Letter to Josiah Quincy, September 11, 1783.
3. Letter to the Editor, *Times Colonist*, August 22, 2003.
4. Center for Strategic and International Studies in Washington, D.C., USA

CHAPTER TEN: GETTING BIGGER AND BETTER
1. Emily Carr, *Hundreds and Thousands: The Journal of an Artist*, Irwin Publishing, 1966

INDEX